LOOKING BEYOND:

A SOUVENIR OF LOVE

TO THE

BEREFT OF EVERY HOME.

BY J. O. BARRETT.

Better, my friend, I feel the daisies growing o'er me. KEATS.

Let the light enter. GŒTHE.

BOSTON:
WILLIAM WHITE AND COMPANY,
"BANNER OF LIGHT" OFFICE,
158 WASHINGTON STREET.
NEW YORK AGENTS: THE AMERICAN NEWS COMPANY,
119 NASSAU STREET.
1871.

Stereotyped at the Boston Stereotype Foundry,
No. 19 Spring Lane.

DEDICATED

TO

MY ANGEL MOTHER.

DEAR READER:

Herein you will find a "Sunny philosophy," — "a balm for every wounded heart." Its sweet truths, and its consoling revelations from the "better land," will be needed by all. For we are all journeying thither, and do ask for light to shine upon the way. Mine is humble, — but a single ray, — while the great sun of heavenly benediction remains unmeasured. I may show you, perhaps, where its founts of divine baptism are. "Come and see."

I am indebted to many friends, and especially to Mrs. Sarah C. Dunbar, of East Boston, Mass., for facts herein stated. A thousand thanks.

That we all, as witnesses of the truth, may have a candid hearing, and that the inspirations we here have breathed, may enflower the path of every bereft heart, is the sincere prayer of your

Faithful Brother,

J. O. B.

GLEN BEULAH, WIS., July, 1871.

CONTENTS.

LOOKING BEYOND.

LIFE'S MYSTIC KEY.

> "O Bearer of the Key
> That shuts and opes with a sound so sweet!
> Its turning in the wards is melody!"

ALIVE is even the crystal — one of our mother's tears. All is life. The minerals, metals, vegetations, animals, soils, waters, atmospheres, are bundles of life. The microscope reveals an infusorial world — living creatures in corals, in drops of water, in flakes of snow, in grains of sand, on every leaf a colony, grazing like oxen upon a meadow, and in the mold of decaying bodies a forest of beautiful trees, with the branches, leaves, flowers, and fruit. "There exists no dead anatomy; what seems to be such is only another body."

O for an acoustic instrument, that we may lay our ears upon the growing or dying grasses and insects, upon thoughtless brains and pulseless hearts, and hear the sweet melodies at these feasts of joy!

Nothing is without its use. Down in the sea's deeps are the rarest pearls; under the mountains are the purest silver and gold; under the ice is the crystal current; under the mantling snow are embosomed germs of plants and flowers. In time they come forth — born again — more beautiful for the destructions whence they are developed. If the angry waves and floating weeds dash against the fish in ocean, lake, and stream, scales and shells are formed to protect these happy tribes. If wind and frost chill the tender shoot of the tree, they harden a garment of bark, that says to the heart within, "Lie still, my darling; all is safe; I gird you round." How we love the sweet, white lily! Let us be grateful for the mud in which it was rooted and fed, for the ripples that cradled it, for the sunlight that wooed it forth in summer — the fairest flower in the world.

On every plan of being Nature climbs to perfection. Says Hudson Tuttle, in his Arcana, "Nature, by one plan ever pursued, seeks one grand and glorious aim — the illumination of an immortal intelligence. From the chaotic beginning, through the monsters of the primeval slime, through all the evanescent forms of being, up to man, that plan has been undeviatingly followed, and that aim held in view. Without this attainment creation is a gigantic failure, and the results are objectless combinations of causes. The great Tree of Life strikes its roots deep into the soil of the elemental world, and stretches up its branches into the present. Its perfect fruit is Man, immortal in his spiritual life."

Never die the souls of the species. These shall remain in their integrity forever. Am I not nature, and nature I? I breathe upon a rock, and a part of myself is there invisibly crystallized; upon a leaf, and I am *in* the leaf. The touch of hearts marries them, and the pulse is different. A particle of water in the ocean is a distinct individuality, unlike the rest: dissolve it into hydrogen and oxygen, or analyze each of these, — if it be possible, — and in essence it is yet the same. Bring the electric battery, and it is water again. What if I be dissolved? Am I lost? Is there an outside to the universe? Be, then, afraid of nothing. What combines all should be master. As said the wise Brahmin, "Make pleasure and pain, gain and loss, victory and defeat, the same, and then prepare for battle." With the power of God, what chance is there for death? Blot it out forever! "There was no beginning, and lo! also, there is no ending!"

I find myself in everything. I am enveloped in the aura of the universe. I am traceable to atomic affinities — the rock my brother, the plant my sister; every motion, every sensation, every coloring is in me represented. I have life-webs inwoven with all the past, threading out into the future, all planes of being touched, in the infinite climbing. Does matter then ultimate in spirit? As well ask, Does spirit ultimate in matter? How can the ever-changeable reach an ultimate? Buzurgi, the Persian poet, tells the whole story: —

"What is the soul? The seminal principle from the loins of eternity.

"This world is the womb; the body its enveloping membrane.

"The bitterness of dissolution Dame Fortune's pangs of childbirth.

"What is death? To be born again, an angel of eternity."

The progressive arc is the material side — matter refining; the descending arc is spirit enveloping itself in it — taking up to itself to make our world the "image of the heavenly." Sphere within sphere! How far up the chain of being? Ask the soul — ask angels!

Formation and growth are through the conjunction of two forces — feminine and masculine — negative and positive — centripetal and centrifugal. Buds, flowers, fruit, all forms, are the children of this union. Qualitatively is combined in one what there is in two. The individual is the social in epitome. Hence affiliation into marriages, families, societies, nationalities.

Soul is the maternal, molding force; spirit is the quickening, electrifying force. The *principles* are reciprocal — bride and bridegroom, mother and father — never twain, but one personality, inseparable as love and thought.

As the feminine and masculine principles, fecundating the plant, sip up elements of vitality through the medium of the roots and leaves, culminating in flower and seed, so soul and spirit, conjointly acting as the builders, form the spiritual or celestial body through the medium of the physical — the fruit of the spirit, the residence of the angel within. Thus the spirit changes houses. The new is the "house of many mansions." Says the Brahmin Seer, in the *Bhagvat Geeta*,* —

* Written by an ancient, learned Hindoo, based upon a then popular system of religion, recognizing Brahm as Deity and Kreeshna as the second incarnate Deity. The ancient Hindoos were a polished

"As a man throweth away old garments and putteth on new, even so the soul, having quitted its old mortal frames, entereth into others that are new."

Physical surfaces are spiritual centers. Nature forms her perfections in highest latitudes. The coarser material is nearer the center. Rocks are down deep in the earth. On its surface are the verdure, flowers, birds, beasts, air, sunshine, the most active electricities, and man the coronation of all. A rightly-constructed dwelling is most beautiful in its upper stories; its foundation is rock, lying on the ground. The roses are not on the roots, but on the tips; and the highest on the bush, having the most sunshine, are the sweetest and fairest. Electricities act upon surfaces. The dome of the sky is above us, curtained with blue, red, and golden clouds by day, and bright stars by night. Central in our bodies are the coarse-fibered organs. The bones, which are lowest down, are hard and crystallized; nearer the surface are the finer organs. The nerves, and all the senses, have keen sensation on the surfaces. So the beautiful embodiment of the spirit is the blossoming forth of this physical body — the immortelle of life. Epes Sargent, author of "Planchette," quoting the basic argument of Allan Kardec, says, "The spirit body is no more the spirit than the body alone is the man; for the spiritual body can not think; it is to the spirit what the body is to the man, the agent or instrument of his action. The human form and that of the spirit body

nation. The Bhagvat Geeta is characterized, symbolically, with deep spiritual thought. It has been republished from an English print by the Religio-Philosophical Publishing House, Chicago, Ill.

are identical; and when the latter appears to us, it is generally with that particular exterior with which we were formerly familiar."

The celestial body is nurtured by the elemental pabulum of the spirit world — atmospheres, and fruits, and drinks — analogous with this world. Already we are beginning to discover what provision we must make to grow and sustain this "house not made with hands."

Every organ of our being contributes something of its own nature to the development of its spiritual body — organ for organ, hand for hand, brain for brain, heart for heart, circle for circle, to a completeness, having all we are now, represented in more beautiful form — the man perfected. According to this ratiocination, if the body is more animal in its functions than intellectual, passional than moral, so is the spiritual organism. A defective tree has defective fruit. A bitter fountain sends forth a bitter stream. As all there is of the body, even to habits, are nurturers of corresponding organs in the spirit body, — allowing latitude for accidents that may not essentially mar the balance and beauty of the transmission, — the law of duty to organize and preserve this body in temperance and purity is most solemnly imperative. Since lust, and gluttony, and intemperance, and selfishness, and jealousy, and slander, and uncharity, poison and slime the functions of the body and its senses, so the spirit body, deriving thence its supplies for building, out of diseased materials, becomes correspondingly dark — an advance, but comparatively an ill-shaped and unhappy home. The truth of this law is severely moral; and how does it warn us what habits we cultivate, what associations we seek, what opinions we entertain! Everything of this kind, good or evil, right or wrong, pure or impure, holy or unholy, enters materially into the composition of the spirit organism, and there is no possible escape. A single thought, or deed, or habit, may warp the spirit for ages; or, if orderly and true to Nature's law, advance us into ages of progress. As a healthy root makes a beautiful tree, as a love-child becomes a golden character in after years, so a good motive, a temperate life, a habit of charity, or a thought of holier conditions rising into ambition, incidentally engenders a glorified spirit body for the *angel* spirit to live in. We are building every moment of our lives on earth, not only character, but our immortal house. Which shall it be, dark or light, deformed or beautiful, happy or unhappy, discordant or angelic?

With outer vision we see our physical body; why not with inner vision see our celestial body? — *body*, not the *spirit*. Is the *spirit ever* seen? May be the super-archangels can even *see* soul and spirit, the *essential principles* of all being; but media, generally, see *only symbols* of the spiritual, — others the light or spheres of the celestial bodies, — others see *these* organisms as they are in their divine beauty, but not yet the spirit within. As the celestial is a real organism, it certainly comes under the comprehension of the spiritual senses. Here is an objective world of causation, and we live in it! What we see is simply the picture of the object. The medium between the spirit and body is the system of nerves. Wherever a nerve is, is spirit. By this the spirit has sensation and consciousness with its surroundings. It is the telegraph of the spirit, and brain is its battery. Rays of light are the undulating carriers of the image of an object to the optic nerve, and then, by a beautiful chemistry, analogous with photographing, it is impressed where the mind catches it up into living consciousness. Here is a mystery, standing out as a fact for analysis. Now, when a subject is psychologized completely, his sphere, senses, will, and mind are, so to speak, swallowed up by the operator. They are *en rapport* with each other, when every emotion and thought of the controller is felt by the negative. It is the same as though they two were one brain and one affection. The subject sees the same pictures, or hears the same sounds trembling in the sensorium of the operator, whether it be a real image of an object and impression of melody, or a mental conception of such. Doubtless the chemical action of the one brain upon the other is analogous with that of light, since the results are the same.

Now, there is *spirit* light. Moses saw it in the "burning bush," Ezekiel saw it as "the appearance of the likeness of the glory of the Lord," Jesus saw it as a "transfiguring cloud;" our media see it flooding all our earth as "the sun of righteousness." By it our spiritual photographers are taking the likenesses of departed friends; and angelic psychologists picture upon mediumistic brain the scenery of the immortal spheres.

A. A. Wheelock, in an editorial to the "American

Spiritualist," speaks of Mrs. R. Robinson, of Oswego, N. Y., who, years ago, was mentally and physically prostrated from the effects of reflection upon the monstrous dogmas of her church (Catholic), "in which condition spirits were enabled to get control of her organism, causing the body to lie in an unconscious state for three days. So complete was the entrancement, so fully were the outer senses of the body closed, that no signs of life were visible, and preparations were made for the burial of her body."

Saved from premature burial, and true to her enlightenments, she became a Spiritualist; but her sickness totally blinded her outer senses. May be it is but a psychological vail. While thus blind, she sees clairvoyantly persons and objects in the darkest room, and accurately describes them.

The spirit light is musical in its undulations and fragrant from those floral kingdoms. Hence by the psychological agency of a spirit we can sense the aromas of those "paradises of God"; can smell, hear, taste, touch, see the spiritual; and can actually, as spirits, step out from our physical temples without the process of real death. Jung Stilling says, "Examples have come to my knowledge in which sick persons, overcome with an unspeakable longing to see some distant friend, have fallen into a swoon, during which they have appeared to the distant object of their affection."

Professor George Bush, in his "Museum of Wonders," relates several instances — one of a trance medium in Philadelphia, who, at the solicitation of a lady anxious about her absent husband then in London, went as a spirit to that city, found him, and reported certain facts. On his return home, meeting this medium, he averred that he was actually visited by him *in persona* in London, having seen him there that very night.

By the law of psychological sympathy, friends affectionally are a unity. It is very common for the one to know when the other is coming, before they meet. The experience of one affects the other. During our late war, it is said that two brothers, standing side by side on the battle-field, fell dead at the same moment; but on examination only one was found hit by the bullet. This was death from sympathy. By the same law diseases are communicated, "revivals" carried on, revolutions projected, victories secured. Hence the spiritually-minded obtain news outside of conversation or the mails. All facts in heaven and earth are open as the day to the inner world of the truly mediumistic.

The appearance of apparitions is explainable by this law of sympathy. If a distant friend is soon to depart this life, those who are *en rapport* may receive the news at the time, or even before the event. Our spheres are like sun-rays, reaching ahead, announcing in advance as a telegraph. It is by use of this law that a powerful psychologist controls a variety of media, or that a spirit of this or the angel world will impressionally communicate with different friends at the same moment. As the least particle of lead is a cube and by nature represents the whole mine, so the most refined element of our sphere is ourself in essense, a living prism through which we see our spirit or the spirit of a friend. When Dr. Underhill had thoroughly magnetized one of his subjects, he asked, "What do you see?" "O, wonderful," replied the lad — "a thousand little Underhills on your arm!"

Theodore Parker, since ascended, when in his last earthly moments under the mellow skies of Florence, became conscious of his dual being. "There are two Theodore Parkers, the one here sick and struggling, the other at work at home." There was a friend reading at the time one of his great sermons in Music Hall. There *were* "two Theodore Parkers" — the shadow and the substance.

On the lonely sea, earth-life seems lost behind the shrouds of mystic reverie. The thought of the great deep beneath us! — how solemn, too, the calm heavens and watch-stars above! how trustingly the soul drifts out to the "shining shore" on each widening wave! Then we are spiritual in our meditations. Then spirits, haunting each ship and steamer, manifest themselves in ways so weird, so protectingly!

Robert Dale Owen, in his "Footfalls on the Boundary of the Spirit World," informs the reader, by evidence of a number of reliable witnesses, of Robert Bruce, first mate on board a bark trading between Liverpool and St. John, New Brunswick, who saw a stranger in the cabin writing at a desk on a slate. His gaze was solemn and steady. No one on board could account for this visitation. The captain, with the mate, soon after descended to the cabin. Not a soul could then be found. On the slate, in a strange handwriting, was the order, "*Steer to the nor'-west!*" Testing the chirography, no one on board wrote the same. Curiosity excited, the captain changed the ship's course accordingly, and in a few hours rescued a vessel, with a large number of passengers, from imminent wreck. There the mate met again the very stranger — one of the imperilled voyagers!

"It seems," exclaimed the mate to the captain, "that was not a ghost I saw to-day, sir; the man's alive."

"What do you mean? Who's alive?"

"Why, sir, one of the passengers we have just saved is the man I saw writing on your slate at noon. I would swear to it in a court of justice."

"Upon my word, Mr. Bruce," replied the captain, "this gets more and more singular. Let us go and see this man."

They found him in conversation with the captain of the rescued ship. They both came forward, and expressed in the warmest terms their gratitude for deliverance from a horrible fate — slow-coming death by exposure and starvation.

The captain replied that he had but done what he was certain they would have done for him under the same circumstances, and asked them both to step down into the cabin. Then, turning to the passenger, he said, "I hope, sir, you will not think I am trifling with you; but I would be much obliged to you if you would write a few words on this slate." And he handed him the slate, with that side up on which the mysterious writing was not.

"I will do anything you ask," replied the passenger; "but what shall I write?"

"A few words are all I want. Suppose you write, '*Steer to the nor'-west.*'"

The passenger, evidently puzzled to make out the motive for such a request, complied, however, with a smile. The captain took up the slate and examined it closely; then stepping aside, so as to conceal the slate from the passenger, he turned it over, and gave it to him with the other side up.

"You say that is your handwriting?" said he.

"I need not say so," rejoined the other, looking at it, "for you saw me write it."

"And this?" said the captain, turning the slate over.

The man looked first at one writing, then at the other, quite confounded. At last, "What is the meaning of this?" said he; "I only wrote one of these. Who wrote the other?"

"That's more than I can tell you, sir. My mate here, says you wrote it, sitting at this desk, at noon to-day."

The captain of the wreck and the passenger looked at each other, exchanging glances of intelligence and surprise; and the former asked the latter, "Did you dream that you wrote on this slate?"

"No, sir, not that I remember."

"You speak of dreaming," said the captain of the bark. "What was this gentleman about at noon to-day?"

"Captain," rejoined the other (the captain of the wreck), "the whole thing is most mysterious and extraordinary; and I had intended to speak to you about it as soon as we got a little quiet. This gentleman," pointing to the passenger, "being much exhausted, fell into a heavy sleep, or what seemed such, some time before noon. After an hour or more he awoke, and said to me, 'Captain, we shall be relieved this very day.' When I asked him what reason he had for saying so, he replied that he had dreamed that he was on board a bark, and that she was coming to our rescue. He described her appearance and rig, and, to our utter astonishment, when your vessel hove in sight, she corresponded exactly to his description of her. We had not put much faith in what he said; yet still we hoped there might be something in it, for drowning men, you know, will catch at straws. As it has turned out, I cannot doubt that it was all arranged, in some incomprehensible way, by an overruling Providence, so that we might be saved. To him be all thanks for his goodness to us."

"There is not a doubt," rejoined the captain of the bark, "that the writing on the slate, let it have come there as it may, saved all your lives. I was steering, at the time, considerably south of west, and I altered my course for nor'-west, and had a look-out aloft, to see what would come of it. But you say," he added, turning to the passenger, "that you did not dream of writing on a slate?"

"No, sir. I have no recollection whatever of doing so. I got the impression that the bark I saw in my dream was coming to rescue us; but how that impression came I cannot tell. There is another very strange thing about it," he added. "Everything here on board seems to me quite familiar; yet I am very sure I never was in your vessel before. It is all a puzzle to me. What did your mate see?"

Thereupon Mr. Bruce related to them all the circumstances above detailed. The conclusion they finally arrived at was, that it was a special interposition of Providence to save them from what seemed a hopeless fate.

During the late rebellion, Geo. Jones, of Burlington, Wis., a soldier, being then in Philadelphia, whilst lying in his bunk, saw a pale light approaching, which increased in volume and intensity, and opened close to his pillow, when lo! there reclined, as in a sick attitude, his little boy Oliver, then only four years old. The father, though filled with a heavenly joy, was apprehensive that his boy was soon to die. It was afterwards ascertained by a letter from his wife, that at that very hour of visitation — three o'clock in the afternoon — Oliver had been wrapped in a deep slumber in his cradle at home in Burlington; rousing from which he called his mother, saying, "O, mamma, I've seen papa — I did see dear papa!" In a few days, by diphtheria, the child was taken higher.

Professor W. D. Gunning furnishes the readers of his "Is it the Despair of Science?" with the following proof of our duality of being: —

"A few years ago, Mr. H., the father of my informant, was captain of the ship Ann, which was owned in Richmond, by a Mr. Robinson. Captain H. was sailing from Richmond to Rio with a cargo of flour. The Ann had passed the capes of Virginia, and was going along smoothly with an eight-knot breeze, when Captain H. turned in to sleep. It was the first night out, and between twelve and four o'clock, when he dreamed that he saw Robinson, the owner, standing beside his berth, dressed as usual, in a long black coat. He woke, thought nothing of the dream, and dropped to sleep. He dreamed the same dream again. He awoke a second time, and thought it a little strange that Robinson, in that long black coat, should haunt his dreams. Again he dropped into a sleep, and a third time dreamed the same dream. When he rose in the morning, he observed strange movements among the crew, who were colored men. He called the mate, and asked what was the matter with the men. 'Why, sir,' said he, 'a ghost was seen here last night.' 'A *ghost!*' said the captain: 'tell me what he looked like.' 'Well, sir,' replied the mate, 'he was a tall man, dressed in a long black coat, and he stood at the leeward gangway. He looked just like Mr. Robinson.' 'Did any other person see him?' asked the captain. 'Yes, sir,' said the mate, 'the whole watch saw him.' The captain called the watch, and examined the men separately. Each man testified to having seen the ghost, and said that it wore a long black coat, and stood at the leeward gangway, and looked like Robinson. The Ann made a quick passage to Rio. No letters awaited the captain. The flour was sold; he started for home, and, in due time, the Ann was again off the capes of Virginia. When the pilot-boat came alongside, Mr. Ramsey, the pilot, broke the news to the captain that Robinson was dead; that he died the first night his ship was out; that his mind, to the last, was on the ship."

"The following incident happened to an elderly lady friend," says H. Scott, of Lancaster, Ohio, "who is of a high order of intellectual culture, and may be accepted as entirely accurate in every particular. She is an honored member of an Orthodox church. She had a brother residing in a city more than two hundred miles distant, whom she had not seen for some time. At about three or four o'clock in the morning he stood before her in her bedchamber, robed in sleeping clothes. The sister was greatly pleased, and said, '*Brother, is this you?*' or '*Brother, I am glad you have come.*' He replied in a brotherly way, and, after some further interchange of words, he was gone. I inquired whether she had thought it a dream only, and whether she had had a consciousness of having passed from the sleeping to the waking state. She replied that it all seemed very real, and that she had no doubt it was the spirit of her brother. She said he appeared twenty years younger than he really was, and then called my attention to two portraits of him, which were hanging on the wall of the parlor, one of which was taken twenty years before the other, and was the one which represented him as she saw him in the vision, and caused her to say, '*Why, brother, how young you look!*' Within a couple or three days she received a letter giving some of the particulars of her brother's death at about the hour she had seen him. She answered the letter, and spoke of her dream or vision; and in return, it was written that the brother seemed to have passed away for several minutes, and they had thought all was over, when he again partially revived and turned his eyes upon those about his bed, while a pleased expression lit up his face, but he did not speak, when his spirit took its final leave. She believed that during that brief interval of seeming death he was present with her. The letter also said that, after he was '*laid out*,' he appeared twenty years younger than when alive."

"A touching story," says The Revolution, "is told of a young sister of Alice and Phœbe Cary, whose early death was deeply lamented by her friends. A few weeks before her departure, and while she was still in health, she appeared for some minutes to be plainly visible in broad daylight, to the whole family, across a little ravine from their residence, standing on the stoop of a new house they were then building, though she was actually asleep at that moment in a bedchamber of the old house, and utterly unconscious of this 'counterfeit presentment' at some distance from her bodily presence. This incident is said to have given the sisters a strong interest in the phenomena of 'Spiritualism.'"

All nature is a unit: all forces blend, as do drops in the ocean. Does not a touch upon any part of the human body affect the whole? Does not a little thought communicate itself to every nerve in the system? So in the outer world — a common bond of sympathy is there. A wave of a lake, a slight zephyr, makes a motion through the great whole. Commensurate with its power, nothing is circumscribed in influence.

Then a spirit is virtually present wherever any of its acts or relics exists, or its sympathy extends. Take a bar of magnetized steel; divide or subdivide; each piece is a distinct magnet. Separate them ten feet, a hundred, a thousand, a mile, any distance; do we thus destroy the reciprocal relation? Not at all; they imperceptibly respond. Mind is just as inseparable from its history. Between the mind and its sequences is an eternal union. What is memory but the registry of thought? Nothing is lost here. Its record-leaves are endless; and every thought, every emotion, every act, every event, is indelibly impressed; the chemistry of circumstances will at some time call it up in review. Persons resuscitated from the drowning state aver that the experiences of life flash before them in a moment. What a solemn truth is here — what a serious examination at the judgment hour of memory some time to be! How pathetically plead the very hours we live, to dot upon the soul beautiful deeds! Nothing then is plainer than that we *never* can be separated from each other. All is one vast immortality. What if we pass away into the realm of spirit; the memory lives and brightens with use, and the sympathy is stronger than before, for the heart yearns after its counterpart to meet externally as they *constantly* meet internally. The separated spirit lingers in love with all the objects it has lived with. Yesterday the sun bathed all the landscape in light, and every particle of ground and drop of water was fused with its golden magnetism. Was the sympathy destroyed when the sun went down? Everything turned a face sunward, seeking it, and in the effort to get close to it, crowding its fellow forward, there is a circuit of the earth round and round. So reciprocal is this love, our mother-world is ever blooming and fruiting with dissolving views of beauty. A lock of hair — electric medium for the brain — is not only a remembrancer, but is an affectionate tie, tinged with the lingering divinity which the departing felt at the first glimpse of heaven. This even brings the angel nearer.

Time and distance cannot separate friends that love. The space between is larger room for soul to meet its soul in sympathy. The spirit and earth worlds, correlated as soul with body, are mutually dependent. Can the planets revolve and develop forms of life without the sun, or the sun perform its functional duty without the planets? The veil is there between the two worlds, and "is getting thinner," exclaims Rev. Nehemiah Adams. Says the Swedish seer, "If angels and spirits were to be removed from a man, he would instantly fall down like a stock or a stone; and they, on the other hand, could not subsist, if they were deprived of their support and resting-place in mankind."

"In the brain of man," says Professor Draper, "are impressions of whatever he has seen or heard, of whatever has been made manifest to him by his other senses; nay, even the vestiges of his former thoughts are stored up." All true in experience, and as we make the test, we discover our mental impressions are immeasurable; that the sensitive plate of the brain has caught its picturings from millions of beings, seen and unseen; that under the watch-lights of some heavenly guardian, we can read events in the realm of subtile causes, ere they have descended into our practical world; that, as we drift out on the ocean, tides of mentality, conscious or unconscious, wakeful or asleep, our souls, agitated by each pulse-wave of life, by dream or vision, or feeling, or sign, or hearing, find the "Isle of the Blest," — our home-land of birth and destiny, where innumerable angels meet us in loving fellowship.

Margaret Fuller Ossoli, the sweet spirit that since often visits our sorrowing world, had a presentiment of her fate ere she launched upon the stormy ocean from Rome to America. "Various omens," she writes, "have combined to give me a dark feeling. . . . In case of mishap, however, I shall perish with my husband and child." The waves were their graves. Her prayer was fulfilled — "Ossoli, Angelo, and I may go together!" Who writes this horoscope? who but an angel can premonish us of the seeming fatality that lifts us higher? The instances are common with the spiritually illuminated when the angels visit their "chosen ones," even at a time of health, to prepare them for the change, when those heavenly visitants are sure to come again and take them home.

The Lockport Journal, N. Y., in 1865, relates what a minister said at the funeral of a little boy: "Several weeks before his death, while his cheeks were yet ruddy and his eyes bright with the lustre of health, he came down from his sleeping room in the morning, and told his mother he had just seen the most beautiful lady he ever saw, and that she was very anxious that he should accompany her away to a beautiful land. The little boy felt somewhat inclined to listen to the persuasive pleadings of the beautiful lady, but finally told her that his mother could not spare him, and he must be excused. In about three weeks the same vision was repeated, only with more clearness and beauty. The mother endeavored to persuade her little boy that he had been dreaming, but he could not believe this, asserting that he really saw the beautiful lady, and that her persuasiveness was almost irresistible. In about three weeks the 'beautiful lady' appeared the third time, and renewed her earnest entreaty for the company of the little boy. He used the same child-like argument this time, asserting that his mother could not spare him. In about three days from this latter interview the little boy was taken sick, and very soon died."

A lady in New York had in her family two Irish servant girls, who were sisters, very much attached to each other. One of them was suddenly taken ill. "A few days afterwards, and while suffering under the prostrating effects of her disease, she beckoned her sister to her bed, and whispered in her ear, 'Bridget, I am going to leave you; mother and sister Bessie (spirits) have just been here, and they told me they were coming after me in a few days, and that they would take me with them.' She accordingly died within a few days from that time."

Herman Snow, of San Francisco, California, formerly a Unitarian clergyman, accompanies a brotherly note with the following: —

". . . And now, as I write, comes up in my memory the venerable form of my noble father, whose earthly home was in Pomfret, Vermont. In his early years he was considerably under the influence of the old order of religious thought, but being somewhat impressible, and otherwise mediumistic, he was one of the earliest of his neighborhood to welcome the light of modern spritualism; and thus, although even then far advanced in years, my respected father was not long in emerging from the shadows, so that the lingering darkness of a confused and irrational theology no longer obscured the clearness of his spiritual vision. The firmness with which he embraced the new faith was owing largely to the fact that a little grandchild, only about seven years old, and who had never learned to write, was developed into an exellent writing medium, and from day to day gave characteristic messages from departed friends, often in a very close *fac simile* of their handwriting.

"A few years previous to his departure, when at about the age of eighty, my father had an attack of an acute disease, so severe that, for a time, it seemed to be his direct summons to the world beyond. I was absent at the time; but on my return, knowing his cheerful way of looking at the matter, I said, in a somewhat playful mood, while conversing with him upon the subject, 'Well, father, did you get so that you could see over upon the other side?' I will give the reply substantially in his own words. 'No, I did not get so that I could see clearly over to that other side; but I did have something quite interesting and peculiar in my experience. I was lying awake one night at the time my case was considered most doubtful, the door of my room being open into the apartment adjoining. I was trying to make up my mind whether I had rather go or stay; and I had about concluded that, as I had got to be so old, and so many of my friends were already there, I had rather go; when suddenly there came, gliding in through the door, a light and shadowy form, whose features I could not clearly distinguish. Then came another, and another, until some seven or eight had entered the room and ranged themselves around my bed. They waited for a time, as if in consultation, and then went away as they came.'

"From our subsequent conversation I found that my father understood clearly that this was a visitation of dear friends who had come with the probable expectation of being *then* permitted to receive him into their spirit-arms; but on a due observation of the case, they saw that not then, but a few years later, this pleasant office would be theirs. And so they left him for a time, whilst, with venerable grace and dignity, he added a few closing years to a long and useful career. And so it happened. When nearly eighty-three years of age, after a long and tedious confinement, during which came other cheering intimations of the nearness of that band of expectant friends, the still youthful spirit, although lingering painfully in an old and disabled earthly body, finally passed joyfully and triumphantly into the presence of the friends of his early youth."

All *artists* are spiritual; they live most in the inner world of soul — a world more *real* than this earth of rock and land and water — a world where "there are angel faces, and we should see them, if we were calm and holy." Our sister reformers — the Motts, the Ernestine Roses, the Anna Dickinsons, the Susan Anthonys, the Stantons — are all thus gifted and inspired, instinctively in love with this angelic religion. Mrs. Julia Ward Howe gave the following account of the origin of her "Battle Hymn of the Republic" to a Detroit audience, a few evenings since: —

"I was on a visit to Washington, during the first winter of the late war, with Governor Andrew and other Massachusetts friends. We had been spending the day in the soldiers' camps on the Potomac, and I heard the 'John Brown Hymn' sung and played so often that its strains were constantly sounding in my ears. As the words in use seemed an inadequate expression of the music, I wished very much for an inspiration which would provide a fitting rendition of so beautiful a theme. But it did not come, and I retired to bed.

"Early in the morning, before daybreak, I awoke, and my mind, in a half-dreaming state, begun at once to run upon the rhyme of the 'John Brown Hymn.' Very soon the words commenced fitting themselves to its measure, and the lines spun off without further effort. I said to myself, 'Now I shall lose all this unless I get it down in black and white.' I arose, groped about in the dark, got such stationary as may be found in the room of a Washington hotel, sat down, then wrote, as I frequently do, without lighting a lamp, that 'Battle Hymn of the Republic.'"

Lydia Maria Child relates the following: —

"When Harriet Hosmer, the sculptor, visited her native country a few years ago, I had an interview with her, during which our conversation happened to turn upon dreams and visions.

"'I have had some experience in that way,' said she. 'Let me tell you a singular circumstance which happened to me in Rome. An Italian girl named Rosa was in my employ for a long time, but was finally obliged to return to her mother on account of confirmed ill health. We were mutually sorry to part, for we liked each other. When I took my customary exercise on horseback, I frequently called to see her. On one of these occasions I found her brighter than I had seen her for some time past. I had long relinquished hopes of her recovery, but there was nothing in her appearance that gave me the impression of immediate danger. I left her with the expectation of calling to see her again many times. During the remainder of the day I was busy in my studio, and I do not recollect that Rosa was in my thoughts after I parted from her. I retired to rest in good health and in a quiet frame of mind. But I woke from a sound sleep with an oppressive feeling that some one was in the room. I wondered at the sensation, for it was entirely new to me; but in vain I tried to dispel it. I peered beyond the curtain of my bed, but could distinguish no objects in the darkness. Trying to gather my thoughts, I soon reflected that the door was locked, and that I put the key under my bolster. I felt for it, and found it where I had placed it. I said to myself that I had probably had some ugly dream, and had waked with a vague impression of it still on my mind. Reasoning thus, I arranged myself comfortably for another nap. I am habitually a good sleeper, and a stranger to fear; but, do what I would, the idea still haunted me that some one was in the room. Finding it impossible to sleep, I longed for daylight to dawn, that I might rise and pursue my customary avocation. It was not long before I was able dimly to distinguish the furniture in my room, and soon after I heard familiar noises of servants opening windows and doors. An old clock, with ringing vibration, proclaiming the hour, I counted one, two, three, four, five, and resolved to rise immediately. My bed was partially screened by a long curtain looped up at one side. As I raised my head from the pillow, Rosa looked inside the curtain, and smiled at me. The idea of anything supernatural did not occur to me. I was simply surprised, and exclaimed, "Why, Rosa! how came you here when you are so ill?" In the old familiar tone to which I was so much accustomed, a voice replied, "I am well now." With no other thought than that of greeting her joyfully, I sprang out of bed. There was no Rosa there! I moved the curtain, thinking she might perhaps have playfully hidden herself behind its folds. The same feeling induced me to look into the closet. The sight of her had come so suddenly, that, in the first moment of surprise and bewilderment, I did not reflect that the door was locked. When I became convinced that there was no one in the room but myself, I recollected that fact, and thought I must have seen a vision. At the breakfast-table, I said to the old lady with whom I boarded, "Rosa is dead." "What do you mean by that?" she inquired; "you told me she seemed better than common when you called to see her yesterday." I related the occurrence of the morning, and told her I had a strong impression Rosa was dead. She laughed, and said I had been dreaming it all. I assured her I was thoroughly awake, and in proof thereof told her I had heard all the customary household noises, and had counted the clock when it struck five. She replied, "All that is very possible, my dear. The clock struck into your dream. Real sounds often mix with the illusions of sleep. I am surprised that a dream should make such an impression on a young lady so free from superstition as you are." She continued to jest on the subject, and slightly annoyed me by her persistence in believing it a dream, when I was perfectly sure of having been wide awake. To settle the question, I summoned a messenger and sent him to inquire how Rosa did. He returned with the answer that she died that morning at five o'clock.'"

The Scranton (Pa.) Republican tells the following sad story of one of the victims of the late Pittston disaster: "William James expired about three o'clock on the afternoon of the Tuesday following the catastrophe, and was the last added to the list of those upon whom the death-angel laid his hand in that awful havoc. He was a Welshman, and had been in this country about seven months. On the morning of the dreadful day in question he had taken his breakfast, and his wife had made ready his dinner and set the pail beside him. For some time he sat wrapped in thought, his arms folded, his eyes fixed vacantly upon the stove, and a deep melancholy apparently brooding over him. He was aroused from his reverie by his wife telling him that his dinner was ready, and that he would be late, as the bell had rung. He started to his feet, and gazing upon her for a moment with a look full of tenderness and significance, said to her, 'If I should not come back alive would you be in such a hurry getting me out?' The wife answered, 'No,' but remarked that 'if he was going at all, it was time he was gone.' He lifted his pail without saying a word, and after kissing his wife, kissed his four little children, who were sitting playing on the doorstep. When he had got about fifty yards from his home, he returned again, and kissed his wife and children once more with great fervency. His wife noticed that he was the victim of gloomy forebodings, and as he turned away she was about to entreat him not to go to work if he apprehended any danger. But hope and courage and the necessities of their family overcame her intention, and she let him go. She stood in the door, and watched him on his way to the fatal pit. When at a point where he turned out of her sight, he paused and cast a wistful look towards his home and little ones, and seeing his wife, waved with his hand a last adieu."

Are there not sentinel angels standing on the watch-towers of Life intently noticing our steps and perils, and warning us by a thousand ways of impending misfortunes? Were we prompt to obey our "first impressions," how much of sorrow we might avert! When we are more spiritual, deeper imbued with faith in the "divine overshadowing," with obedience to the laws of our being, with consecration to spiritual experiences, temptations can be resisted and dangers averted. How many on sea and land have been rescued from peril by spirit impressions! As an instance among the great number may be mentioned that of Judge O. P. Poston, a prominent lawyer of Kentucky. After relating reliable tests of spirit-guardianship, he thus speaks of his warnings and deliverances from perils during the late war: —

"In the earlier part of the rebellion, many of my friends and myself made an earnest effort to stay the progress of secession in Kentucky, and became more or less obnoxious to the opposite faction. I always escaped capture during the repeated raids made into the State. I was always 'warned by dreams' that were singularly vivid, and sometimes repeated the same night of the approaching foe, and I left the night previous to the arrival of the band. On Christmas morning, 1863, I sat at my office table alone, writing notes on business, and as I sealed the first letter, a spiritual voice, clear and distinct, said to me, 'The rebels are about!' and, as I continued to write, it was repeated four times before I took my horse and left for the country. At that time the weather was cold, and no rebel forces were in Kentucky. General Baird was at Danville, ten miles south of my locality, with ten thousand Union troops. I never felt safer than on that morning; yet at that time General Morgan was eighteen miles west of our town with two thousand rebel cavalry. They thus kept inviolate their promise made to me in the earlier part of the war, and warned me of all approaching danger."

Love is health; and love lives by exchange of spheres. This is the law of healing by the laying on of hands. So strong is this cord, it can sometimes bring the spirit back to live for years in its "clay tenement," even after a transit "across the river." What but this that could say, with fulfilment in its command, "Lazarus, come forth!" that returned the son of the Shunamite woman? that, by touching the bier, "the dead sat up and began to speak"? . . . "Folded eyes seek brighter colors than the open ever do."

"We should see the spirits singing
  Round thee, were the clouds away;
'Tis the child-heart draws them, singing
  In the silent seeming clay, —
Singing! Stars that seem the sweetest
  Go in music all the way."

The instincts of some people, even without philosophy, have instituted what seems to be superstitious notions, but which are in fact based in spiritual law. A touch or a tear, or a yearning affection, may keep back the departing spirit.

"In some parts of Holland, when a child is dying, persons shade it by their hands from the parents' gaze; the soul being supposed to linger in the body as long as a compassionate eye is fixed upon it. Thus, in Germany, if he who sheds tears when leaning over an expiring friend, or bending over the patient's couch, does but wipe them off, he enhances, they say, the difficulty of death's last struggle."

"A few months since," says S. B. Brittan, in his admirable work, entitled 'Man and his Relations,' "an eminent Presbyterian divine, in New York, was borne by disease to the very portals of the invisible world. He had a distinct consciousness of his condition. Veiled in light, his spirit rose and hovered over the body. He could distinctly see the wasted form, stretched on the couch beneath him, pale, pulseless, and cold, but his immortal self was thrilled with inexpressible peace and joy. Just then his wife, to whom he was tenderly and strongly attached, called to him, with the deep earnestness of that undying love which can endure all things but separation from the object of its devotion. The potent magnetism of that loving heart counterpoised the combined attractions of the spheres, and even recalled the unshackled spirit from the heavens just opening to receive it. He returned to the body. The next moment a gentle voice — calling his name in mingled tenderness and grief — vibrated on the outward ear, reminding him that he was still a dweller in the earth."

The Memphis Whig publishes the facts of a case in point. While the wife was bending over the apparently lifeless form of her husband, "she bathed the brow with her scalding tears, and fervently kissed the frigid lips. In this great struggle love triumphed over death. . . . That man recovered, and with his wife soon left Memphis, inspired with the new energy of returning health, and emotions of grateful reverence towards the Being in whose hand are the issues of life."

About ten years since, Miss Kate Marshall, of Hingham, Wis., with other girls, one evening went in bathing into a pond near the village. It being quite dark, she ventured beyond her depth and sank to the bottom. The alarm was given amid screams and cries, when Edward Hobart, hearing the news, rushed from his home, dashed into the water, and by sense of feeling found the body and brought it to the shore, then apparently dead. By rolling the body, pressing the lungs, breathing into the nostrils, rubbing upwards, and other expedients, she was resuscitated. Afterwards relating her sensations, she said "she was so happy then; that she saw her body distinctly down in the water, and had no desire to be returned into that prison, as it appeared.

She was with the angels, and dreaded the effort to find the spot where lay the pale casket. She instinctively tried to baffle the searchers, but the moment her body was touched by Mr. Hobart her *spiritual* consciousness was lost amid the most excruciating agonies, as her spirit struggled to get possession again of its former residence."

What to us is death, is emancipation to the spirits. Their return to their bodies, as in trance conditions, is *really* like the death so many dread. This is the general testimony of trance mediums. When once amid the beauties and serenities of the "better world," the thought even that they must return produces a chill. "O, that we could stay!" is their universal exclamation. This is the experience of Dr. E. C. Dunn, and other trance mediums.

Hudson Tuttle, in his "Arcana of Nature," gives an incident of his own clairvoyant experience. "I apparently," he says, "left the body, and in company with my guardian, went to the spirit-world. I knew I must return. I came to my body. I saw it cold and motionless, rigid in every muscle and fibre. I endeavored to regain possession of it several times, yet could not, and became so alarmed that I could not even make the effort; and it was only by and through the influence of the friends who were present that I succeeded at all. When at length I did recover my mortal garb, the anguish, the pain, the agony of that moment was indescribable. It was like that which is used to describe death, or which drowned men tell us of when they at length recover."

Professor Helmholtz announces, as the result of some recent experiments made by M. Baxt, that the excitation of the motor nerves is greater in summer than in winter. As death is a cooling process of the body by the withdrawal of the spirit, the "manifestation" of the clairvoyance or clairaudience of the departing, will be more or less dim and feeble, just in proportion to the frigidity of the body. It can be readily seen how difficult it is for a spirit to return to its body, that is, in the trance or cataleptic condition, and the solemn duty on our part to be cautious and patient lest we be guilty of murdering the innocent by a premature burial. Where the "silver cord" is not severed, as in a trance, it is impossible to prevent the return of the spirit. The discovery of its peril creates the very condition that drives it back; and then the agony is terrible, unless we who survive understand our business, and endeavor to aid the frightened friend by gentle manipulations and tender, long-suffering sympathies.

The great utility of cultivating mediumship is illustrated in the case of a mother and child in Canada, showing also the culpability of hasty burials. Mariette Westover was then six or eight years old. The child sickened, and the witnesses said "died," and declared "she must be buried." A spirit was able to impress the mother that her child was *not* dead. She battled against the asseverations and importunities of the friends, keeping the little body five days, when lo! the child-spirit returned, to the supreme joy of all.

"On the exhumation of the Cimetiere des Innocents at Paris, during the Napoleon dynasty, the skeletons were, many of them, discovered in attitudes struggling to get free; indeed some, we are assured, were partly out of their coffins. So noted was this matter in Germany, as to give rise to a custom of placing a bell-rope in the hand of a corpse for twenty-four hours before burial.

"Miss C. and her brother were the subjects of typhoid fever. She seemed to die, and her bier was placed in the family vault. In a week her brother died also, and when he was taken to the tomb, the lady was found *sitting in her grave-clothes*, on the steps of the vault, having, after her waking from the trance, died of terror or exhaustion.

"A girl, after repeated faintings, was apparently dead, and taken as a subject into a dissecting-room in Paris. During the night, faint groans were heard in the room; but no search was made. In the morning it was apparent that the girl had *attempted to disengage herself from the winding-sheet*, one leg being thrust off from the trestles, and an arm resting on an adjoining table.

"The emperor Zeno was prematurely buried; and when the body was soon after casually discovered, it was found that he had, to satisfy acute hunger, *eaten some flesh from off his arm.*

"A romantic story is told of a young French lady at Paris, bound to a hated marriage, while her heart was devoted to another. She fell into a trance, and was buried. Under some strange influence her lover opened her grave, and she was revived and married. Dendy tells a story of another strange lady, who was actually the subject of an anatomist. On the existence of some faint signs of vitality, he not only restored the lady to life, but united himself to her in marriage.

"Bourgeois tells that a medical man, in 1838, from the sudden influence of grief upon the organic system, sunk into a cataleptic state, but his consciousness never left him. The lamentations of his wife, the condolence of friends, and the arrangements regarding his funeral, were all distinctly heard. Perfectly aware of all that was going on around him, he was placed in the coffin, and carried in solemn procession to the grave. As the solemn words, 'earth to earth,' were uttered, and the first clod fell upon his coffin lid, so sudden an influence was produced upon his organic system by terror as to neutralize the effect of grief — he shrieked aloud, and was saved."

Through the agency of a society instituted in Amsterdam, in 1767, to resuscitate drowned persons, one hundred and fifty, in a brief period, were rescued. Similar societies have been formed in Milan, Hamburg, Venice, Paris, London, Glasgow, and should be in all the principal cities in the world. Dr. George Watterson, in Sartain's Magazine, cites to ninety-four cases of premature burials in France prevented by fortuitous circumstances. One of the first objects of such associations should be to inquire into the secret laws of spirit and life, and the causes of suspended animation. The sepulture of the living is horrible. Indifference here is an "unpardonable sin." Where so many these times are subject to trances, we cannot be too vigilant. Ere the body is buried, we should be sure it is dead. The almost universal practice of burying the so-called dead within three days, is reckless and unpardonable. The time required for the spirit to extract from its body all that belongs to it, varies according to constitutional compactness, or the closeness of relation between the inhabitant and its house. It may be in one, two, three, or five, or more days. It is longer when the spirit is forced out by accident, more especially so at times of vigorous health. An intelligent German girl, living in 1869 near Burlington, Wis., having had a severe attack of the measles, had a warning of her departing, and told her father not to "hurry in her burial." Her body remained in a warm room, lifeless to appearance, but undecayed, for three weeks, ere decomposition would warrant interment. It cannot be too earnestly repeated, *Cultivate mediumship, to know when the spirit has fully departed from its earthly house.* The nature of the disease and the age of the person should be considered. Symptoms of decomposition are safe criterion. Some one says that iron or steel in a living body will oxidize; in a dead body will not. Sudden draughts of fresh air have been known to revive the body; also, raising it from its recumbent position, and frequent and spasmodic charges of electricity.

THE NEW BIRTH.

"Go, give to the waters and to the plants thy body which belongs to them: but there is an immortal portion; O Djatavedas, transport it to the world of the holy." — *Rig Veda.*

"IS there not a balm in Gilead? Is there not a physician there?" The dark side of life is the bright side. Every night has a star of Bethlehem. There is a sweet oasis for every weary pilgrim; a Bethesda in every bereft heart; an angel in every sorrowing home; night for the dews; clouds for the rainbow; winter for the beautiful snow; frost for the outbursting of buds into trees and flowers; pains of body for birth of soul; earthly loss for eternal gain; sickness for calmer converse with heaven; bereavement for ascension to holier life. Then let us wing the hours with immortal hope.

By a delicate experiment, it is ascertained that sensations are transmitted to the brain with a rapidity of about one hundred and eighty feet per second, or at one fifth the rate of sound. The brain requires one tenth of a second to transmit its orders to the nerves which preside over voluntary motion. To transmit an order by the motor nerves to the muscles till they act, requires two tenths of a second. If, then, the nerves are decayed, or clogged by bad habits, or inflamed as in brain fevers, the communication between the inner and outer life, or capacity to *manifest* what the spirit is cognizant of, is of course intercepted; so that the spiritual vision or hearing by the natural senses will be mixed or indefinite. Hence the vague and wandering ideas some have in their last hours. They indicate the struggle of the spirit, however; and were the obstructions removed, or the nervous channels open, we who remain would behold positive revealment of immortality. One's habits very much modify spiritual identity. "Temperance in all things" is a "passport over." Though we come into this world crying, we should go out of it rejoicing.

There are floods and ebbs in our tides of being. The transit-hours are the most imminent. "The least mortality," says a writer in the Quarterly Review, "is during the midday hours, namely, from ten to three o'clock; the greatest during the early morning hours, from three to six o'clock. . . . The hour after midnight is the lowest maximum."

Does the measure of human life depend on physical strength? As often do the frailer remain, while the vigorous suddenly pass on. By strict obedience to the spiritual laws of mediumship the dial of our life may turn back even ten degrees. Disdaining green fruit in their paradises, transported from earth-lands, the angels are patient for the "ripening," and demand of us patient labor and waiting till we have *earned* the right to the "Eden above." Many a spiritually-minded man and woman has felt the springs of rejuvenated health from the ministering angels, to endure yet longer for the good we do.

There is an unerring ratio between the growth of the

physical and celestial bodies. If the one is slow to maturity, so is the other. Some trees develop sooner than others. So of plants, so of animals, so of humanities. The life of some is short because the spirit is swift in unfolding. Mourn not because the golden tulip comes and goes so early, while "the last rose of summer" is late in the season. Soonest in blossom is soonest in fruit.

The analogy which Mrs. E. O. G. Willard, in her science of "Sexology," traces between the two births, is finely drawn: —

"When the soul has obtained its centralization and its spiritual organization under the cover and protection of its physical garments, then, by shaking off these garments, it emerges from its chrysalis state as free in space as the planet on which it had its birth. . . . As the physical birth of the fetus is death to its uterine envelope, so a spiritual birth is death to its physical casket, the body; or, as the destruction of the uterine casket in which the child is developed implies the birth of the physical system, so the destruction or death of the physical body implies the birth of its spiritual system. As the destruction of the uterine casket does not destroy the physical form that it has helped produce, so by analogy the death of the human casket cannot destroy the spiritual form that it has helped to develop. As the physical birth of the child does not destroy the transmitted parental impression upon its features, much less should a spiritual birth destroy the impressions it has received through the senses of its physical parent, the body, inasmuch as the soul is incomparably finer in its texture, and must therefore be much more tenacious of impressions than the body."

In his "Death and After Life," depicturing scenes and occupations in the "Summer Land," A. J. Davis, basing his conclusions upon spiritual observation, thus describes the process of transition: —

"Suppose a human being lying in the death-bed before you. Persons present not seeing anything of the beautiful processes of the interior, are grief-stricken and weeping. This departing one is a beloved member of the family. But there, in the corner of the room of sorrow, stands one who sees *through* the outward phenomena presented by the dying one, and what do you suppose is visible? To the outward senses the feet are there, the head on the pillow, and the hands clasped, outstretched, or crossed over the breast. If the person is dying under or upon cotton, there are signs of agony, the head and body changing from side to side. Never allow any soul to pass out of the physical body through the agony of cotton or feathers, either beneath or in folds about the sufferer.

"Suppose the person is now dying. It is to be a rapid death. The feet first grow cold. The clairvoyant sees right over the head what may be called a magnetic halo — an ethereal emanation, in appearance golden, and throbbing as though conscious. The body is now cold up to the knees and elbows, and the emanation has ascended higher in the air. The legs are cold to the hips, and the arms to the shoulders, and the *emanation*, although it has not arisen higher in the room, is more expanded. The death-coldness steals over the breast, and around on either side, and the emanation has attained a higher position nearer the ceiling. The person has ceased to breathe, the pulse is still, and the emanation is elongated and fashioned in the outline of the human form! Beneath it is connected the brain. The head of the person is internally throbbing — a slow, deep throb — not painful, but like the beat of the sea. Hence the thinking faculties are rational while nearly every part of the person is dead! Owing to the brain's momentum, I have seen a dying person, even at the last feeble pulse-beat, rouse impulsively and rise up in bed to converse with a friend, but the next instant he was gone — his brain being the last to yield up the life-principles.

"The golden emanation, which extends up midway to the ceiling, is connected with the brain by a very fine life-thread. Now the body of the emanation ascends. Then appears something *white* and *shining*, like a human head; next, in a very few moments, a faint outline of the face divine; then the fair neck and beautiful shoulders; then, in rapid succession, come all parts of the new body down to the feet — a bright, shining image, a little smaller than this physical body, but a perfect prototype or reproduction in all except its disfigurements. The fine life-thread continues attached to the old brain. The next thing is the withdrawal of the electric principle. When this thread snaps, the spiritual body is free, and prepared to accompany its guardians to the Summer-land. Yes, there is a spiritual body; it is sown in dishonor and raised in brightness. . . .

"At the battle of Fort Donelson, I saw a soldier

instantly killed by a cannon ball. One arm was thrown over the high trees; a part of his brain went a great distance; other fragments were scattered about in the open field; his limbs and fingers flew among the dead and dying. Now what of this man's spiritual body? I have seen similar things many times — not deaths by cannon balls, but analogous deaths by sudden accidents or explosions. Of this person whose body was so utterly annihilated at Fort Donelson, I saw that all the particles streamed up and met together in the air. The atmosphere was filled with those golden particles — emanations from the dead — over the whole battle-field. About three quarters of a mile above the smoke of the battle-field — above all the 'clouds that lowered' upon the hills and forests of black discord, there was visible the beautiful accumulation from the fingers and toes and heart and brain of that suddenly killed soldier. There stood the new spiritual body three quarters of a mile above all the discord and din and havoc of the furious battle! And the spiritual bodies of many others were coming up from other directions at the same time; so that from half a mile to three and five miles, in the clear, tranquil air, I could see spiritual organisms forming and departing thence in all directions."

J. W. Seaver, of Byron, N. Y., in a letter of July, 1871, substantiates the statements of other media respecting the transition from the "shell" to the priestly robe of an angel: —

"Some ten or twelve years since, at Byron, N. Y., our beautiful sister, Miss Jane Dodge, aged about sixteen, after a painful illness by consumption, was brought to the trying hour, when the realities of this transition must be met. It was in the spring-time of the year, when the atmosphere was perfumed by the sweet breath of flowers, on an early Sabbath morning, when the friends of the family were called to witness the approaching dissolution. Among others in attendance were my wife and Mrs. Belfy, and her young daughter Henrietta, who was seven or eight years old. From the time when Jane was first 'struck with death,' as the saying is, until the last evidences of animation were given by her body, some three hours or more had passed, near the close of which, completing the new birth of her spirit, Henrietta requested the attention of my wife aside; and when they were withdrawn to a remote part of the room, or to an adjoining bedroom, she informed her that she could see the spirit of Jane just rising and forming above her head, as she lay upon her dying couch."

Henrietta had for some time past given evidence of possessing mediumistic gifts. That she would, at such a solemn hour, in the presence of death (which usually is so terrible to children), attempt to practise deception upon a lady of mature years, is entirely beyond the region of probability; besides, she could have known nothing about the philosophy of death.

Mary Carpenter, in a letter addressed to Joseph Baker, of Janesville, Wis., thus describes the transition of her mother, January 28, 1852: —

"Her last words were addressed to me. Perceiving that she was dying, I seated myself in the room, and was soon in the state of spiritual clairvoyance. With the opening of the inner sight, the painful scene of a mother's death was changed to a vision of glory. Beautiful angelic spirits were present, watching over her; their faces were radiant with bliss, and their glittering robes were like transparent snow. I could feel them as material, and yet they communicated a sensation that I can only describe by saying, it seemed like compressed air. Some of these heavenly attendants stood at her head, and some at her feet, while others seemed to be hovering over her form. They did not appear with the wings of fowls, as angels are commonly painted, but they were in the perfected human form. They seemed so pure, so full of love, that it was sweet to look at them as they watched the change now taking place in my mother.

"I now turned my attention more directly to my parent, and saw the external senses leave her. First the power of sight departed, and then a veil seemed to drop over the eyes; then the hearing ceased, and next the sense of feeling. The spirit began to leave the limbs, as they died first, and the light that filled each part in every fibre drew up towards the chest. As fast as this took place the veil seemed to drop over the part from whence spiritual light was removed. A ball of light was now gathering just above her head, and this continued to increase as long as the spirit was connected with the body. The light left the brain last, and then 'the silver cord was loosed.' * The luminous appear-

* Professor Schiff, experimenting upon nerve actions by means of thermo-electric needles, discovered that the life of the brain does not cease immediately after the cessation of the circulation; that the elevation of the sensory nerves could be produced for twelve minutes after the entire cessation of the beating of the heart.

ance soon began to assume the human form, and I could see my mother again. But, O, how changed! She was light and glorious, arrayed in robes of dazzling whiteness; free from disease, pain, and death. She seemed to be welcomed by the attending spirits with the joy of a mother over the birth of a child. She paid no attention to me or any earthly object, but joined her companions, and they seemed to go away through the air. I attempted to follow them in the spirit, for I felt strongly attracted, and longed to go with my mother. I saw them ascend till they seemed to pass through an open space, when a mist came over my sight, and I saw them no more. I returned, and soon awoke, but not to sorrow as those who 'have no hope.'

"This vision, far more beautiful than language can express, remains stamped upon my memory. It is an unfailing comfort to me in my bereavement. Her death was a great loss to me, but I cannot lament it. O, it is a glorious change to her!"

Thomas L. Harris, in the Spiritual Telegraph, describes the beautiful transition of his wife to the realm of spirits: —

"On Tuesday evening, at about six o'clock, the spirits of her relatives, in company with other spirits, to the number of about thirty, entered the room, and while she was apparently asleep, formed a circle around the bed. I was placed at this time, by their influence, in a deep interior condition, retaining, however, full possession of all the external faculties and powers. From the moment this circle of spirits was formed she became free from all pain.

"We watched the ebbing life of the external form till about a quarter before twelve (midnight). Gradually we felt the pulse sinking to rest. At that time a sudden light, like a diffused silver radiation, came and rested upon her face. A wondrous smile played upon her countenance. Such divine love, such ineffable peace diffused itself, melting into light in the air around her, that she seemed transfigured, and changing into an angel before our sight.

"As her eyes began to close, kneeling by her side, I inclined my face to the pillow by her cheek, and laid my arm over her form. Heavenly bliss filled all the internals of my mind, and I passed at once into *rapport* with her spirit. Gradually I felt her spirit-form arising from the external. As it arose my own arms were lifted by it. I saw a vortex, or spiral of white light, narrowing to the diameter of about two feet, just above her body, and opening above it into the SPIRITUAL WORLD. In this vortex were innumerable angelic forms, and as she entered the spiral, they lifted her from my arms. She disappeared in that transcendent light."

The Telegraph adds, "The spirit had departed, and only the form — still beautiful in its decay — remained to gaze upon. Refusing the repose which protracted wakefulness and physical exhaustion had rendered necessary, the watcher still continued his vigil through the long night, and morning found him by the remains of his beloved Mary. When it was light her spirit came to him, and while her form was distinctly visible, she gave him a communication, closing with these words: *Mary's dear love to all.* NEVER MORE BE AFRAID TO DIE."

William W. Barrett, and wife Addie, then residing in Anoka, Minn., were called to assist the transition of a little son of Jay Fuller, some time in the summer of 1869. The scene occurred at the residence of Mrs. Lepper; who, being in the clairvoyant state, saw the "silver cord" flickering forth from its panting body attached to the beautiful little spirit. As these friends pathetized the child, the cord would seem to roll up and recoil, then come out again. Mrs. L. saw it at length attenuate at its attachment, finer and finer, till every sparkle of light had gone; and then the attendant matron-angel embosomed the dear one for their loving nursery amid fadeless flowers.

Let us not infer from such perception of celestial bodies, when passing from the old to the new, that there is an *unmaking* or dissolving process, as if the spiritual were at first disintegrated. Structural disorganization never precedes birth in any department of nature. When the grain, or the bird, or the animal is developed, it comes forth organized in perfect shape. Nature never retrogrades. A spirit is a wholeness, having an organized personality, *fac-simile* of its earthly house, but far more beautiful. As its capacities show, it can step out of its present body, as in trances and apparitions, before it takes a final leave; and certainly death can have no power to dissolve it for a reconstruction, when its only office is to set the spirit free. The acorn drops from the burr, the apple from its parent tree, the child from its mother's womb; so the spirit casts off its garment and puts on the "white vesture;" gathers up from its former house all the essences of life it can appropriate and from the spiritual atmospheres, till it — the spirit as such — is clothed with a body once terrestrial but now *celestial*. If the intelligence of the departed is active at the time, the process is more easy in drawing up the robes of spiritual life; if inactive on account of weakness, ignorance, or insensibility, spirit friends tender their assistance, taking off earth's robes as a mother would a child's on going to rest. This undressing and thence redressing in the vestments of the spiritual, is as beautiful as that of the chrysalis that drops its shell and comes forth in the gaudy plumage of the butterfly.

Nor should we infer from appearances that the struggles of the departing are always agonies. No doubt a natural death, when we have lived out our allotted time with faithfulness, is serene as the ascent of fragrance from the flowers; easy, as Mr. Dorsey said of Henry C. Wright's departure, "as a child falls to sleep upon its mother's breast;" but when there is a premature departure, as by accident or pestilence, there must necessarily be a conflict. But it *may* not even then be painful. When a spirit takes possession of a medium, there is, generally, at first, — ere the medium becomes accustomed to the influence, — a contortion of the muscles; but the sensation is far from agony; it frequently is most pleasurable. Death is a similar operation, only a reversing of the action under the same clause. Whilst the body is struggling, the spirit may be rejoicing. Are not the fledglings and the parent birds so happy when the shells are broken? It is birthday in the nest! *There* is singing — not crying.

Dr. Dewey grows rapturous over it: "Hour of release from life's burden — hour of reunion with the loved and lost! . . . What longings, what aspirations, bathed in the still night beneath the silent stars!"

Grace Munson was about eleven years old. When her body was in apparent intense agony, her spirit, unconscious of this external life, was engaged in play with angel children, often speaking of and to "Josie," her cousin who had passed before her. Seeing a spiritual house building, she said at the rising sun, "Now I am at home!" and to her home she glided.

A departing believer was asked, in the midst of convulsions, "Are you in pain?" and the reply, almost with the last breath, was, "It is delightful!"

Dr. Cullen, when departing, is said faintly to articulate to one of his friends, "I wish I had the power of writing or speaking, for I would describe to you how pleasant a thing it is to die."

Keats, a little before he passed over, when his friend asked him how he did, replied in a low voice, "Better, my friend. I feel the daisies growing over me."

Schiller, when ready to go, was asked how he felt. "Calmer and calmer," he replied.

"*It will be a wedding rather than a funeral*," said Edward Haynes, of Dorchester, Mass. Then hearing spirit music, with a smile he glided "out on the sea of eternity." "*A deep content — a sublime pleasure — all is well*," said "Father Henshaw," the Quaker Spiritualist. "The passage is bright as sunshine!" said Helen Barton. "Wife, I shall be with you in a few moments!" said Oliver Peabody, of Lunenburg, Mass., just as he caught a glimpse of his companion awaiting his arrival "beyond the flood."

"Let us go up there, mamma," said little Ida Graves, only six years of age, when sickness was preparing her for the journey. "Go where?" asked her pensive mother. "Why, up there," reaching up her hands with ecstasy. Ida saw the white robed angels, and *such* beauty!

Laura de Force Gordon says of Mrs. Mary Leroy, Golden City, Colorado, who departed April 29, 1867: "When suffocating for breath, she whispered, 'O, I am the happiest being in the world! My body suffers but my spirit is at peace.'"

Laura Cuppy, speaking of Olive C. Blowers, of Woodland, Colorado, says, "Her last moments were illuminated by spiritual light; her last words were, 'How beautiful!' and, holding her husband's hands, she passed from death to life without a struggle."

Up among the back hills of Maine, writes A. E. Frye, lived a poor family; the parents were addicted to drink. The oldest son suddenly died. The younger brother was so sad; but he seemed to catch a new light somewhere, and he went to work, and earned the title of "Little Basket Maker." Some angel told him he would soon be "sick and go to heaven." He told Mrs. K. (the kind farmer's wife who adopted him) about "dying;" and when the sad hour came, he said, "Brother Joseph is here!" So the "Little Basket Maker" clasped hands with his spirit brother, with a soul so beautiful, so happy!

If death is such a joy, as so many witnesses aver, it

becomes us who remain not to lessen it by mismanagement. It has been ascertained, by experiment, that changing the "battery" from one room to another may neutralize the "manifestations." If the germ of the welcome child is jarred in its "holy of holies," it is more or less injured. The process of the "new birth" is more delicate still. Sad looks, groans, sighs, wringing of hands, and loud moanings agitate the soul, retard its emancipation, and cloud the spiritual vision. How can the dear departing see angels under such smothering sorrow, or hear their sweet voices amid so unpardonable confusion?

The room for the loved one should be sacred to neatness, order, purity, and stillness. The bed or couch should also be specially prepared for the auspicious event. It is birthday! If cotton or feathers to lie on are not fit for the living, they surely are not for the "dying," so called. They invariably smother the spirit as well as body. Be calm. The place is holy! Angels are there! Bend low and tenderly for that loving "good by;" then stand a little distance away from the parting friend, unless a nearer position will relieve suffering or aid the sublime process. Let the kiss be electric with hopeful love. Give words of cheer; invoke divine benedictions; suppress loud sobbing; though tears fall, hold the heart-springs with a firm trust in God; look up to see the new-born pilgrim of eternal years; sing inspiring songs about the blessedness of the life to come. Our spiritual songstress, Emma Tuttle, tells us what to sing *then:* —

"O, let no sobs of woe bewail me when I die,
But sing to me, and let me rise exulting to the sky;
Mark not the damp of death which gathers on my face,
But sing in joyful melodies of God's sustaining grace.

"Mark not the fading eye, nor yet the lines of pain,
But sing of those immortal shores where I shall live again;
Sing of the shining ones who passed death's gate like me,
And triumphed o'er the lonely grave, immortalized and free.

"Like music low and faint my soul shall float afar,
And wake in heaven, delightful heaven! where God's sweet singers are.
O, not with burning tears of those who love me best,
But with the ecstasy of song folding still hands in rest."

Feel now the pressure of the hand that seals the undying soul to its own; hear the whispered "adieu" that blends with the angels' welcome; see the heavenly smile chiselled on the fleshly marbled face, playing there at evening sunlight. Blessed calm!

"How many to-day," says Emma Hardinge, "pass from the earth with smiling faces, because their dying eyes are gazing into the bright and beautiful land, and so there is no tear, no sigh, no evidence of grief upon the face of the dying. Is it not because they perceive the presence of the spirits, and know that there is no death, that there is no separation? that in that better life the chain of affection and love is not broken? They perceive that there is no bereavement to the spirit; it is only for us, whilst we remain here. Whilst we are here we feel sorrow and anguish. But we should remember that the love that binds man to man — that divine element that God has written in the human heart — is immortal."

"There is in love
A consecrated power, that seems to wake
Only at the touch of death from its repose,
In the profoundest depths of thinking souls,
Superior to the outward signs of grief,
Sighing or tears. When these have passed away,
It rises calm and beautiful, like the moon,
Saddening the solemn night, yet with that sadness
Mingling the breath of undisturbed peace."

This soul-love, sometimes without our volition, can bring back our beloved to its shattered tenement, just a moment, to speak to us from the "other side," in the assurance of immortality. The transition is gradual; even after respiration has ceased, and every function stopped at the fountain, the spirit may for days and weeks retain some connection with the body. A touch even may chain the departed, moving again the machinery in this earth-life factory that weaves garments for the spirit, when lo! the Christ of the resurrection! If the "silver cord" is not broken, and there is any health left on which to build, love with faith may restore the dying one, when it descends from the ministering angel of God.

About sixteen years ago, Mrs. Ellis, of Genesee, Wis., lay upon her couch in a dying condition. Hands and feet were cold as ice; the nails of the fingers had turned purple, the neighbors and relatives had gathered to witness her departure. When standing there, deeply touched with sympathy, Mrs. B., wife of B. P. Balcom, Esq. (a brother of Mrs. Ellis), was most powerfully influenced by a spirit. It burst like a sunbeam from a dark cloud; she stretched forth her hands, and cried, "O Christ, come and heal this woman!" Mr. Balcom was also charged with healing power, and touched his sister with the same commanding will. The dying woman heard and felt; the electric soul of heaven itself descended into the chilled fountains of life; she exclaimed, "He's come! he's come!" and immediately rose up, stood upon her feet, took a bath, was dressed, and in half an hour walked forth into the yard filled with the astonished people, supported arm in arm by her brother and sister. "O, how beautiful!" she shouted; "all things are in a blaze of divine glory!" She recovered, and is now an aged mother, almost ripe for the "coming harvest."

The following is from the pen of J. M. Peebles, containing an extract from a letter addressed to him by Mrs. Baily, wife of the deceased. Whilst it shows, as in other instances, that a loving hand may hold back the receding spirit, even when its form is tenantless, it opens to view the joy or good man has when his spiritual vision is opened: —

"A Universalist clergyman, Rev. J. W. Baily, of Lima, N. Y., I knew long and well; in fact, we had prayed and preached side by side many a time in years agone; but he had passed on — and Mrs. Baily, his wife, wrote me, giving me an account of his last hours.

"The day before he passed he began to sing, and would sing for hours. Mrs. Baily asked him, 'Does it not tire you to sing so much?' 'O, yes,' said he; 'but I'm so happy — happy, I can't help it.' He then turned his eyes to his daughter Emma, and said, 'Do not weep for your father, dear child, for he is going so happy, —

going home. One by one we pass away; pass to meet in the Father's mansion.'

"She says he then turned his eyes upward, and O, how glorious they looked! They seemed illumined with heavenly light; but he stopped breathing. I laid my hand upon his shoulder. He opened his eyes, and smiled on me, and said, 'Why, I thought I had gone to the spirit world. I have seen over the river, and I can now see on both sides. It is beautiful on this side; but O, glorious, glorious on the other! Why, I see Ellen! I see so many friends there, over the river, and they beckon, beckon to me. I see more, vastly more on that side than I do on this.' Mrs. Baily adds, 'He then pressed my hand, said "do not grieve," smiled, waved his hand, and passed on.'"

S. W. Jewett, writing from California, March 10, 1871, relates this incident: —

"It is eighteen years since myself and Mary K. Jewett were attending, as 'watchers,' at Weybridge, Vt., in the sick chamber of Henry W. Hagar. About eleven o'clock at night his spirit seemed to have taken its flight. Dea. Elijah G. Drake and wife were also present. The Hon. Edwin Hayward was called in to assist. Henry was pronounced 'dead' by his wife, children, mother, and all present. I tried to console them by saying 'he still lives.' The body was silent and motionless for one half hour. Myself and wife remained beside the corpse; we discovered a slight motion of the lips, and called the attention of the family and others to the fact, and remarked, that if Henry could speak, he would tell of visions in the spheres. His first and only words were,

'O, how happy! O, how happy I am! Such heavenly scenes as I have witnessed! I would give all the world to return again to the angelic visions, and experience such happiness once more.' These were his last and only words spoken that evening. In a brief period the body lay a lifeless corpse, to be no more vivified. The spirit left without a struggle."

E. J. Shellhouse, writing from Roseville, Cal., speaks of a brother, and the scenes accompanying his ascension, in 1848, from Colon, Mich.: —

" . . . At last, on the evening of the 8th of June, at about eight o'clock, he passed through, what we supposed, his death struggles. The physician, standing by the bedside, carefully examined his patient, and pronounced him 'dead.' At this moment, my oldest brother stepped forward, and placing his hands under the shoulders of the dying brother, raised him to a sitting posture, and loudly and repeatedly called his name. Calmly he opened his eyes, and, for the first time in three weeks, he spoke rational words. 'Why did you call me back?' he exclaimed in a clear and firm voice. 'I was just going, and you called me back. O, what beautiful music I have heard, and such scenes, more glorious and beautiful than anything I ever imagined in my life. And such throngs of people, with many of whom I am acquainted.' After giving repeated descriptions of what he had seen and heard, he said, 'I will go at three o'clock in the morning,' which he repeated frequently during the night. Just at three o'clock in the morning he became silent, and passed on to the scenes he had described, without even the movement of a muscle."

That very night one of the two sisters was entranced, when she had a vision of her departed brother, saw him plainly, and the very beauties he had described.

John A. Perry, of Elkhorn, Wis., states that when Mrs. Bunker, wife of Alex. Bunker, of Troy Centre, both Quakers by birth, was dying in her good old age, her son all the while held her hand; she ceased to breathe; the pulse was silent; but in a few moments she returned in a gentle manner, opened those eyes again, moved those pallid lips, saying, "O, Nathaniel, why did you call me back? I have been to heaven! Why did you call me back?" What a tangible proof of the identity of spirit, and of the law of love, that by the touch of a hand we may for a moment at least unloose the bands of death, let in the light into the chamber once more, to hear the voice of our beloved this time speaking as an echo from the heavenly home. That son, greeting his mother once more, and that father and sister, and other friends, hearing the familiar words, said sweetly another "good by," and she was free forever.

A lady friend relates the circumstance of her mother's sorrow over her daughter. She would not, could not give her up. The last breath heaved and died away as a zephyr, and the exclamation, "She is gone!" fell so heavy upon the mother, that she wrung her hands, and said so pleadingly, "O, my child, come back! come back!" The child heard, a gentle wave of life swept over the form again, the spirit entered the body, the pale lips moved, the glazed eyes opened, and she whispered "Mother!" and instantly departed. That familiar word touched the mother's soul yet deeper, and she prayed for death to deliver up its prey, when, lo! the spirit obeyed the summons to give one more glimmer of undying affection. This going and coming were repeated to the third time, when the daughter, gathering then all her strength, turned to her weeping mother such a pleading look, saying, "O, mother! I have been with the angels. I am wanted there. Will you not let me go?" That look, and that plea, were sufficient. The mother said, calmly, "Go, my daughter, to your joy, and bid me come when I am ready."

It may be wise, under certain conditions, to hold the hand of the departing one. If the friend so doing is calm and prayerful, it may gratefully aid the exit of the spirit. But we should not refuse the heavenly journey when there is no hope of recovery, and longer remaining is a continuation of suffering.

"We grow at last by custom to believe
That really we live:
While all these shadows that for things we take,
Are but the empty dreams which in death's sleep we make.
But these fantastic errors of our dreams
Lead us to solid wrong:
We pray God our friends' torments to prolong,
And wish, uncharitably for them,
To be as long a dying as Methusalem.
The ripened soul longs from his prison to come,
But we would seal, and sow up, if we could the womb.
We seek to close and plaster up by art,
The cracks and breaches of the extended shell.
And in that narrow cell,
Would rudely force to dwell,
The noble bird already winged to part."

A Wisconsin friend, called to the death-bed of a

neighbor, found him struggling to get away. There was no possible chance to restore the dying man. Instantly he was under control of a wise spirit, who caused him to make a few vertical passes with his hands, when the neighbor, giving his mediumistic brother a grateful look, sunk into rest.

If it is "sweet to die," let us be sweet in spirit. When Mirabeau was "passing over," he ordered his friends to pour perfumes and roses over him; and "let me die," he added, "to the sound of delicious music."

At the death of her aged mother, in New York, a Methodist lady, whose name is forbidden here, being under spirit control, could not weep, but clapped her hands, shouting, "Glory to God! mother has arrived."

Mrs. Mary J. Fetherolf, of Tamaqua, Pa., gives this beautiful test of a child's prophecy and spiritual vision: —

"Emma Hendix, who departed on the 14th of December, 1865, was the daughter of Sarah and Daniel Hendix (members of the Evangelical Church), and was nearly ten years old. About three months before her death, whilst in perfect health, she said she would 'get sick and die, and go to her baby brother.' On the day she was taken sick, she said to her father, 'I am going to die.' Two weeks before her departure, she asked him if he did not see the angels. At the same time she asked a neighbor woman whether she did not see the angel on the bureau; and she replied, 'Do you mean your doll?' 'No, no, the *little* angel!' She was clairvoyant a full week. She asked her parents why they troubled themselves to call the doctor, for it was no use, as she was going 'home to the baby.' She many times called the names of her grandfather, grandmother, and 'baby brother,' who had died some time before, and of whom she was very fond while they were living. She would say, 'all here;' and when asked how many, she would answer, 'five, ten, fifteen, twenty, all here again.' Immediately before her death, she called her relatives to her, bade them 'good by,' and said, 'I am going home; they are waiting for me,' and so passed peacefully on, as if just fallen asleep."

Years agone, when a butterfly-boy, the author's mother paled with consumption. She said, "Good by, dear son!" That saying, that kiss, that fond look imaged in my soul! Looking upward, she said, "Angels!" and was gone. O, the sorrow of that moment! for who had knowledge then of this religion? The death messenger came again and again, and sisters passed higher, each beholding "a door in heaven" opened for their reception. Mother then appeared! These bereavements have shaded my whole pilgrimage with a pensive reflectiveness, but they have been clouds of transfiguration, whence a voice has so often spoken, "This is my beloved son!"

"When Edward L. Hilbourne, of Charlestown, Mass.," writes Sarah C. Dunbar, "was 'passing over,' he heard spirit music, and saw a young girl who brought him rare flowers. She was his sister 'Rose Bud,' so called in spirit life, afterwards recognized as such."

Samuel J. May, who has just "ascended in golden goodness," reverting to the dreamy past, recalls the deep religious impression he obtained in early life by the departure of his brother, and the enchantment for all life which that spirit awoke by a subsequent vision. They had slept together, ate together, and were inseparable companions. That dear brother passed on when Samuel was five years old. He says,—

"There lay my beloved Edward, his eyes shut, his body cold, giving no replies to the tender things that were said to him, taking no notice of all that was being done to him or about him. I gave myself up to a passion of grief, not knowing the meaning of what I saw, but feeling that some awful change had come over him. When the room was darkened, and my father and mother were about to withdraw, I begged them to let me lie down with Edward. My importunity was so passionate that my parents were almost afraid, and quite too tender, to withstand it; so I was covered with a shawl, and laid by my dead brother. When left alone with him I well remember how I kissed his cold cheeks and lips, pulled open his eyelids, begged him to speak to me, and finally cried myself to sleep.

"Most vivid is my recollection of the funeral, of the solemn procession to the burial-ground, and of the weeping of friends and relatives. When I saw them take the coffin from the carriage, and carry it off towards the tomb, I insisted upon seeing what they were going to do with Edward. So my uncle, Samuel May, took me in his arms, descended with me into the family vault, and showed me where they had put away my brother. Then he pointed out the little coffins in which were the remains of several of my brothers and sisters, who had lived and died before I was born, and the coffin in which my grandfather was laid eight years before.

"My kind uncle opened one of the coffins and let me see how decayed the body had become, and told me that Edward's body would decay in like manner, and become like the dust of the earth; but while revealing to me these sad facts, he assured me most tenderly that all these departed ones were still living, that my dear brother's spirit was not in the coffin, but was clothed with another and more beautiful body, and living in heaven with God and the angels. I went home in a sort of maze, crying, and asking questions which human wisdom could not answer.

"I remember that my only brother Charles, then a lad of fourteen or fifteen years of age, tenderly took me to his room, lay down with me on his bed, and tried to comfort me and himself by telling me all that he imagined to be true about heaven, God, and the angels, assuring me again, as others had done, that Edward had gone to live in that blessed place, in that happy and glorious company.

"When night came I was put to bed, in the bed where I had so often slept with Edward. Sleep soon came to relieve my young spirit, wearied with grief and strange excitement, and in my dreams all that had been told me, proved true. The ceiling of the room seemed to open, a glorious light burst in, and from the midst of it came down my lost brother, attended by a troop of child-angels. They left him, and he lay down beside me, as he used to do. He told me what a beautiful place heaven was, and how all the angels loved one another. There he lay till morning, when the ceiling above opened again, and the troop of angels came to bear him back to heaven. He kissed me, sent messages of love to father and mother, brother and sisters, and gladly rejoined the celestial company.

"So soon as I awoke and was dressed, I hurried down to tell the family what I had seen, and to give them the kisses and messages that dear Edward had sent them. The remarkable thing about this dream was, that it was many times repeated, that night after night I enjoyed the presence of my brother, that morning after morning I went down to the family with renewed assurances of love from the one who was gone.

"By degrees my grief abated; the loss of my brother was in some measure supplied by other playmates; new things attracted my attention and occupied my thoughts. But I have never forgotten my Edward; the events of his death and burial, and the heavenly vision, are all still vivid in my memory; and I believe the experience had great influence in awakening and fixing in my mind the full faith I have in the continuance of life after death, — a faith so strong, that I do not believe more fully in the life that now is than in that which is to come."

Lydia Maria Child, who was present at the exit hour of Isaac T. Hopper, the Quaker emancipationist, — that good man and true, — says, "Sensible to the last, he wanted his friends to put his form in a white coffin, made of plain boards, and get a poor man to construct it. He heard voices, saying, —

"'We have come to take thee away.'" When no other one was present, he said to Mrs. C., —

"Maria, is there anything peculiar in this room?"

"I replied, 'No; why do you ask that question?'"

"Because," said he, "you all look so beautiful; and that covering on the bed has such glorious colors, as I never saw."

"The natural world," says this author, "was transfigured before his dying senses; perhaps by an influx of light from the spiritual."

Mrs. E. McGraw, of Plymouth, Wis., says that her Methodist father, "just before the dying moment, reached out his hand to a spirit, Thomas Swift, and conversed with him familiarly, as in former years."

Rev. J. G. Bartholomew, in his happy discourse on the death of Rev. D. K. Lee (Universalist), gives this passage: Referring to the love the departed ever cherished for children, he recalls, with joyful emotion, the opening up of the spiritual powers of that revered brother, just as the curtain dropped that hides from the shadows of earth:—

"I do not wonder that in his last moments a vision of children's faces was opened to his soul; I do not wonder that he should say, '*The children, the beautiful children, don't you see them?*' God sends his angels to us in our trying hours, to bring us strength and comfort, and to fill us with their heavenly peace. He sends such angels as the heart craves most to see. And I do not wonder that angel children crowded around his dying bed. There were the children that had gone up from this congregation to join the glorified in heaven; the children in whom he took such interest in life, whose hearts he moulded, and on whose minds he poured the light of truth; the children in whose plays and pastimes he had so often taken part; they came to him in his dying hour to welcome him to their home above."

The Ithacan relates a scene at the death-bed of Kitty Skinner, who departed in Ithaca, N. Y. She was one of the victims of the Lang family poisoning case: "Little Kitty continued to grow worse until between seven and eight o'clock Wednesday night, when her suffering became intense. She could with difficulty be kept quiet, and only by giving a great deal of anæsthetics. All the time she asked for cooling substances, as snow and ice, on account of her burning stomach. At last death came to the little sufferer's relief, but gradually, for after she became easier she could talk. She talked constantly of her relatives, and said she saw 'Bella Lang (who was buried last week), and she had a beautiful white dress, all plaited about the waist and gathered in the skirt.' She said she wanted to be dressed like Bella, she was so beautiful. Not long before she died, in the midst of her talk, she said, 'Papa' (her father was buried on the 23d of January), 'take hold of my hand and help me across.' Between six and seven, Thursday morning, she breathed her last."

J. Raymond Tallmage, of Calumet, Wis., sends this note, illustrative of the fact that mediums are as cognizant of the departure of friends, even when not immediately present, as the natural eye is of material objects. "In the spring of 1858, Charles W. Raymond, of this place, passed to the other life. I was present. A lady in a distant part of the house suddenly started for the sick room, saying, 'Charles is dying!' As she made the exclamation, he looked towards a vacant part of the room with a most pleasant and beautiful expressive countenance, saying, 'She has come for me; I must go!' and fell asleep."

Uriah Roundey, of Spafford, N. Y., speaking of his grandmother, who was ninety years old, and had been blind twelve years, states that just before her exit she lay a long time in a state of "torpor or trance." At last she suddenly raised her head, just as the spirit was leaving, and addressing a friend present, said, "You tell Laurens (her son) I can wait no longer for him; for there comes a band of angels, with my mother, and I must go."

Mrs. H. S. Benjamin, matron of the Wisconsin state prison, relates an instance of the capacity of the spirit to see even when outer vision was blinded by disease. Her beautiful sister, Annie Cook, seventeen years old, unconscious that she was so near her friends from the spirit world, exclaimed, "O, mother, I am blind — I am dying — but I cannot see; how shall I know my father?" The next moment a wave of light fell upon her spirit, and the heavens opened, and there was her dear parent. "O, yes," she said, so calmly, "he *does* know me — I *see* him — he has come for me!" and then all was still.

Charlotte Barron, of Boston, Mass., was scarcely six years old; her mother stood weeping by her side. The little girl caught a light, and when it burst upon her in full blaze, she turned such a look upon her parent, saying, "O, mother — *mother* — I see father!" and her father took her home.

William Shew, of Cordova, Ill., with the respect usual to a soul that loves the spiritual, says that his wife, a few hours before her departure, "saw many cherubs and seraphs, and heard their songs; and afterwards her 'soldier boy,' William, conversed with her till the casket broke."

Rachel Colburn, of Geneva, Wis., seventeen years old, when conscious of death's call, said to all, "Good-bye — come to me. O, yes — I see now; there is Bertha (her sister's departed little child), she can walk now. There is David's father (her mother's first husband, whom she had never before seen), and there is Mrs. French's child. Why, these little babes have silver bells in their hands!"

"Kiss him for me," said Mrs. French.

"O, yes, I will," said Rachel; and the kiss on those spirit lips was so sweet, that earth was forgotten, for she was in heaven!

Mrs. Margaret D. Read, of Salem, Mass., saw a band of angels coming to take her home; it opened, and she shouted "Mother!" and in an instant was gone.

Daniel W. Hull, who administered the consolations of the angels' gospel to the bereft, writes of Dexter B. Palmer, of North Windham, Conn., "Spirits of many who had lived in the neighborhood crowded around his bed, and as his voice died away he was heard to call over the names of those who were receiving him on the other shore."

J. G. Fish, speaking of Mary Arabella Rhodes, of Philadelphia, writes about his interview with her just before her exit. "'Tell the people,' she said, 'I did not die; I only went to the loved embrace of the dear mother and sisters who were awaiting me on the other side. . . . My dear blessed mother and sister came to me so frequently, and talk so sweetly, and tell me they are only waiting for me, and I see them so plainly, and hear them talk so lovingly to me.' "

A lucid writer describes the closing up of this life with Anna P. Hazard, of South Portsmouth, R. I. She had cultivated spiritual affections, and was therefore intromitted into the society of angels: "In a season of great physical distress, she suddenly became quiet, whilst her eyes seemed earnestly peering into vacancy. Gradually all traces of suffering passed from her features, and her face lit up with a radiant smile, as she pronounced the name of 'Mother,' who, with two spirit aunts, became distinctly visible to her, and with whom she now entered into delightful communion. Some time before her sickness she saw in a dream a remarkably beautiful lily, unlike any she had ever seen before, which disappeared upon her reaching out her hand to pluck it, whilst a grave-like looking hole opened in the ground beneath where it had stood. This same lily, for the first time since, was now again presented to her interior vision, and upon her asking her spirit mother if she was to join her soon, she smiled and bowed her head in token of assent. The delightful vision lasted for some twenty minutes, during which period her countenance continued to wear the same joyous expression, whilst with a clear and unclouded intellect she interchanged messages between, and communed alternately with her father and sisters on earth, and her mother and aunts in heaven. She described her spirit friends as being clothed in beautiful but not unfamiliar garments, moving in a surpassingly lovely wilderness of trees and flowers, and enveloped in a golden atmosphere, the mellow tints and softness of which were wholly indescribable."

Rev. W. H. Cudworth (Unitarian), in a lecture delivered in Music Hall, Boston, January 20, 1871, made these statements, so truthfully said and so feelingly enforced: "It is a well-known fact that Governor Brough, of Ohio, had this experience, though not a religious man. He was lying upon his death-bed, and suddenly extended his hand, and exclaimed that he saw the forms of friends around him, and that others were waiting for him on the further side.

"So it was of Senator Foote, of Vermont. He was the Chairman of the Committee of Extension at the National Capitol. He was taken sick, grew hopelessly so, and his friends came around him, bidding him adieu. He expressed a strong desire to look once more upon the dome before he died. They lifted him up, that he might see the wonderful structure towering in the sky, and as he was looking, he suddenly cried out, 'O, how beautiful! the gates are wide open;' and sank back again, exhausted and dying, to enter in spirit through the open doors! I believe in this opening of the vision; the Christian world, also, is full of this faith in the hour of death, yet refuses to acknowledge the conclusions to which such an admission inevitably lead. In so doing, they are not giving Spiritualism fair play. I have just found an extract from the Independent, which I will read as an instance in point:—

"'At the time when President Olin was seized with that illness which was the precursor of his death, his youngest child, a babe of about two years old, was ill and restless, though the parents did not then apprehend a fatal result. The day of discovered danger, the father was walking in the room where his child lay, when the babe suddenly called "Papa!" desiring to be lifted in its father's arms. "Pa, take baby!" Dr. Olin took the child, and walked up and down the room. The child said, "Pa, kiss baby! Mamma, kiss baby!" and, when this was done, looked up and exclaimed, "Now, God, take baby!" and immediately breathed its last in the father's arms. Was not this a ministration from the invisible world? The believing father received it as such, and was comforted. Children and death are divine teachers. "Out of the mouths of babes and sucklings Thou hast perfected praise."'

"A similar experience took place in a Christian family not acquainted with the science or phenomena of modern Spiritualism, in regard to a child who could never remember its mother, who had died before she could remember her. And it was her custom to ask of her friends or visitors: 'Now tell me about mamma;' and she would ask frequently to be taken into the parlor to 'see mamma;' a portrait of her being kept there. The child grew weaker and weaker, till finally she was upon her death-bed, and friends came in to see her pass away. She lay so still that some of those present said, 'She is gone;' and her father went close to her and said: 'Darling, don't you know papa?' No response! He turned away with a sad heart, and said, 'I'm afraid she's gone;' when suddenly she raised her face, illuminated by the light of the celestial world, exclaiming: 'Mother, dear mother!'"

Adin Ballou, speaking of James Arnold Whipple, of Worcester, Mass., a philanthropic brother, thus shows us the pathway whither that patriot entered: "In religion he was a liberalist, verging for years on scepticism, but afterwards confirmed by Spiritualism into the strongest assurance of man's future immortal existence. Even after embracing Spiritualism, he doubted the uses of prayer and personal exercises of pietistic devotion. But under the chastening discipline of sickness, he was fully drawn away from that externalism of feeling into the sphere of child-like docility, contrition, tender-hearted and confiding prayerfulness. It was a blessed unfoldment to him, his companion and friends. Meantime his spiritual vision was opened to behold bright, cheering, consoling spirits from the immortal world, who gathered around his dying bed, and gave him a sweet welcome to the deathless mansions."

When that faithful apostle, L. Judd Pardee, was unwinding from his frail tenement, the spirits wrote to him through a medium, "Fear not; be strong and full of courage; show how a Spiritualist can die. Thy mother and Mary are seated upon the deck of the little boat which is to bear thee to the other shore; it is wreathed with ivy leaves, and all things are prepared for thy reception; a little longer thou must be patient, and then thou shalt be free."

James B. Buffington, of Warren, R. I., says of his sister Amanda, who departed in February, 1869, "Having taken no drugs to stupefy the brain, and no gloomy minister to darken the mind, while friends were standing around the bed in calmness, her eyes brightened, her countenance lit up with a smile, gazing upward. 'What do you see, Amanda?' asked her mother. 'Geraldine!' was the answer. That was our sister, years ago lost at sea."

When the beloved Judge Wheelock, of Rockford, Ill., was ready to exchange worlds, he exclaimed, "What light is that?" On being informed there was no light in the room, he said, "Ah, but *I* see a bright light;" then clasping his hands, he said, "It is all right; I come." Soon he roused up, and said, "Charles! Charles!" His son-in-law, whose name is Charles Lewis, went to him, and said, "What do you want, father? Here I am." He opened his eyes, and cried out with a loud voice, "Charles Wheelock! Charles Wheelock!" and immediately ceased breathing. Charles was a son of his, who died in California some years ago, and from whom the judge had had several communications through different mediums.

A friend thus describes the departure of Mrs. N. O. Pinkerton, one of our spiritual mediums and lecturers: —

"'O,' she exclaimed, 'this is a glorious doctrine to die by, friends; continue in the good work — it will be a great thing if you can only free a few from the shackles of theological dogmas.' She bade the unstable to stand fast, and exclaimed, in transports of rapture and delight, 'This is the best day of my life; I hear the angels singing; I am happy, happy, happy!' To the doubting she said, while her eyes shone with heavenly brightness, 'Doubt no more — I *know* there is a blessed, glorious, eternal life.' After she had taken leave of the many friends who stood beside her, she asked them to sing, and while tears choked their utterance, they sang —

'Joyfully, joyfully, onward I move,
Bound for the land of bright spirits above.'

She clapped her hands for joy, in response to the sentiments of the hymn. 'O, hinder me not, for I want to go home.' 'I'm going.' 'I am almost over the river.' 'The voyage is pleasant.'"

When a spirit is sufficiently strong at its "new birth," and can have a good medium at the moment, the instant it leaves the form there may be a manifestation. A case of this kind occurred February 2, 1871, in Lime Rock, Conn., as related by Joshua H. Rogers, giving names of reliable witnesses. No sooner had his aunt, Lydia Tomkins, "breathed her last," than her own daughter, standing by her side, was entranced by her overjoyed spirit; and there and then spoke audibly, and in so convincing a manner, that instead of appearing a scene of death, it was a "feast of soul." "That is certainly my wife speaking!" exclaimed her husband, with a thrill of rapture.

Mrs. David Wilson was visited by her dear husband, through a medium, "even when his tenantless body lay in the room, in marble coldness."

Rooms where media are, more especially when departing, are Memnons of spiritual music; the very fibres of the walls and furniture are polarized.

"All houses wherein men have lived and died
Are haunted houses. Through the open doors
The harmless phantoms on their errands glide,
With feet that make no sound upon the floors."

John Wetherby communicates this fact as related to him by a Methodist minister: —

"This man's sister had the diphtheria, and died. She had the disease badly — her palate was all gone, and she could not utter a word, and with difficulty even a whisper. Just before dying, she made signs to her mother to go out of the room, who did so, shutting the chamber door. No one was in the room but the dying, speechless girl, when beautiful music was heard in that room. All the family listened to it, some seven or eight, the words thus beautifully sung being 'Fading, still fading,' — a favorite with the sick girl. When the music was over, they opened the door; the girl had a sweet smile, but could not speak, and in a few moments died."

"A good woman," writes Andrew Glendinning to J. Burns's Human Nature, "whom adversity had made homeless, called for assistance at the house of a friend in Greenock, England. Food and shelter were both given; she became unwell, and, in a few days after music was heard in the humble apartment where she lay. The melodious sounds — such as might be produced by several instruments — were wafted across the kitchen in front of the bed. The poor woman remarked, 'You will not be troubled with me any longer; they have come for me;' and so she passed away to the summer land, where want of gold will not deprive her of a suitable habitation."

George W. Wilson writes of Mrs. Joicy Sweet, of Auburn, O., who passed on in November, 1865: "The day before her death she exclaimed, 'There is father!' though he passed to the spirit realm two years ago. Her daughter asked, 'Do you see your father?' and she replied, 'His spirit.' A few minutes later she spoke of hearing 'sweet singing' and 'beautiful preaching.'"

E. W. Stevens, of Janesville, Wis., furnishes this beautiful description of the departure of his aunt, Mrs. Tabathy Wood: —

"While the bloom of beauty was on her cheek, and the loves that had so fondly entwined themselves about her were yet young, the angels came for her. Death insinuated stealthily his icy fingers about her heart-strings, while the gentle wavings of peace forbade her utter a single movement. Lovingly her inner consciousness watched the opening portals. Affection's footsteps fell lightly on the maple floor. Subdued were the tender voices, as they chokingly whispered, 'She is dying.' Night was drawing her sable pall over the departing day, and the curtained windows excluded the gentle starlight. The crimson tide crept back towards the struggling heart. Affection's ear hovered closely to catch the last 'adieu.' Tearful eyes with suppressed breath watched for the last throb of the heart, and felt for the last slight pressure of the hand. But see! She raises those soft eyelids once again, looks inquiringly about the room, and, with much composure, asks aloud, 'Who is it that sings so beautifully?' On being answered, 'No one,' she replied, 'Yes, the angels are singing!' And with a full, clear voice she broke forth in singing with them the tune of 'Northfield' to the hymn beginning,

> 'How long, dear Saviour, O, how long
> Shall this bright hour delay?
> Fly swifter round ye wheels of time,
> And bring the welcome day.'

Then her pure spirit was wafted to heaven, September 20, 1813."

Margaret Howitt, in describing the last hours of Miss Bremer, says, —

"That (Christmas) night she dreamed, as she told us the next morning, of hearing the most glorious music, such as she never heard in reality; now, of a certainty, this music had been realized to her. Soon afterwards she began to speak of death, and said that 'she would like to remain a little longer to finish the work she had begun.' Later on, said she, 'Now I am so tired, that if God were to call me, I am content.' Afterwards she said, as if speaking portions of *inner thought*, 'God's light in Nature! There is something great in the voice of Nature. I have a sense of the Divine Perfection — it is good — it is beautiful!'"

The music she heard was such as charmed the sainted John, when "in spirit on the Lord's day" he heard music in heaven. It was the welcome of angels — prelude to the undying harmonies of the heavens.

Isaac P. Greenleaf, an apostolic brother, writes that Charles Barker, of Exeter, Me., who had learned the way by the spiritual oracles, saw, when passing higher, the "angel band who had come to welcome him to his spirit home, and heard the sweet strains of melody as sung by angel lips, to cheer him in his passage to the better land."

Mons. A. de Beauchesne, of Paris, in a book entitled "The Dauphin, his Life, his Agony, and his Death," thus relates the last scenes on the earthly side of that unfortunate son of Louis XVI. The young prince (about ten years of age), as he lay upon his sick bed, exclaimed that he heard music.

"Gomin, surprised, asked him, 'Where do you hear the music?' 'From on high.' 'How long since?' 'Since you have been on your knees. Don't you hear it? Listen! listen!' And the child raised his failing arm, and opened his large eyes, lighted up with ecstasy. His poor guardian, not wishing to destroy this sweet and heavenly illusion, set himself to listen also, with the pious desire of hearing what could not be heard.

"After some moments of attention, the child started again, his eyes glistened, and he exclaimed in an inexpressible transport, 'In the midst of all the voices I heard my mother's!'

"This word seemed, as it fell from the orphan's lips, to remove all his pain. His contracted brows expanded, and his countenance brightened up with that ray of serenity which gives assurance of deliverance or victory. With his eyes fixed upon a vision, his ear listening to the distant music of one of those concerts that human ear has never heard, there appeared to spring forth in his child's soul another existence.

"An instant afterwards the brilliancy of his eye became extinguished, he crossed his arms upon his breast, and an expression of sinking showed itself upon his face.

"Gomin observed him closely, and followed with an anxious eye every movement. His breathing was no longer painful; his eye alone seemed slowly to wander, looking from time to time towards the window. . . . Gomin asked him what it was he was looking at in that direction. The child looked at his guardian a moment, and although the question was repeated, he seemed not to understand it, and did not answer.

"Lasne came up from below to relieve Gomin; the latter went out, his heart oppressed, but not more anxious than on the evening before, for he did not expect an immediate termination. Lasne took his seat near the bed; the prince regarded him for a long time with a fixed and dreamy look. When he made a slight movement, Lasne asked him how he was, and if he wanted anything. The child said, 'Do you think that my sister has heard the music? How happy it would have made her!' Lasne was unable to answer. The eager and penetrating look, full of anguish, of the dying child darted towards the window. An exclamation of happiness escaped his lips; then, looking towards his guardian, he said, 'I have one thing to tell you.' . . . Lasne approached and took his hand; the little head of the prisoner fell upon his guardian's breast, who listened to him, but in vain. His last words had been spoken. God had spared the young martyr the agony of the dying rattle; God had kept for himself the last thought of the child. Lasne put his hand upon the heart of the child: the heart of Louis XVII. had ceased to beat. It was half past two o'clock in the afternoon."

"Bœhmen passed to the summer land November 18, 1624. Early in the morning he called his loved son to his side, and asked if he heard that excellent music. Receiving a reply in the negative, he directed him to open the door, that he might hear it better. Asking, afterwards, 'What the hour?' he was told 'two'; upon which he remarked that his time was 'yet three hours hence.' When it was near six o'clock, blessing his wife and son, he took leave of them, saying, 'Now I go hence into paradise!' He then bade his son turn him, and with a deep, peaceful sigh, his sweet spirit departed."

Paganini had the most valuable stringed instruments in the world. One of these was very ancient, having but one string. This he patted and hugged as if a sweet child, and for eight hours improvised upon it the most heavenly music; and then fell back in a swoon, for he heard a "new song from the angel choirs," and passed higher at Nice, May 27, 1840.

"When Mozart had given the finishing touches to his wonderful 'Requiem,' his last and sweetest composition, he fell into a quiet and composed slumber. On awakening, he said to his daughter, 'Come hither, my Emilie; my task is done; the Requiem is done — *my* Requiem is finished.' 'O no,' said the gentle girl, the tears filling her eyes, 'you will be better now; let me go and bring you something refreshing.' 'Do not deceive yourself, my love,' he replied, 'I am beyond human aid; I am dying, and I look to Heaven's mercy only for aid. You spoke of refreshment — take these last notes of mine, sit down by my piano here, sing them with the hymn of your sainted mother; let me once more hear those tones which have so long been my solace and delight.' His daughter complied, and, with a voice tremulous with emotion, sung the following·—

'Spirit, thy labor is o'er,
  Thy earthly probation is run;
Thy steps are now bound for the unknown shore,
  And the race of immortals begun.

'Spirit, look not on the strife,
  Or the pleasures of earth with regret;
Pause not on the threshold of limitless life
  To mourn for the day that is set.

'Spirit, no fetters can bind,
  No wicked have power to molest;
There the weary like thee, the wretched, shall find
  A haven, a mansion of rest.

'Spirit, how bright is the road
  For which thou art now on the wing!
Thy home — it will be with the angels of God,
  Their loud alleluias to sing.'

"As she concluded, she dwelt for a moment on the low melancholy notes of the piece, and then turned from the instrument to meet the approving smile of her father. It was the still, passionless smile which the rapt and departed spirit left upon the features."

"THE LAST SHALL BE FIRST."

"Promise to kiss me on the forehead when I am dead — I shall feel it." — *Victor Hugo.*

NOTHING is so beautiful as a virtuous old age. The vine climbs the ruined walls, pendent with mellow grapes — climbs and hangs over the "other side," and the decay that fed the blossoming and fruiting is lost to view. Sweet it is to go hence, after a career of usefulness, conscious of having never designedly wronged a single mortal. It is the foretaste of paradise to come, the glory of life, and the rest of soul. Josephine — wife of the ambitious Napoleon who sacrificed love for power, and therefore fell as a star to rise no more — said to Emperor Alexander, just as she looked up for spirit guidance, "At least I shall die regretted; I have always desired the happiness of France; I did all in my power to contribute to it; and I can say with truth to all of you now present at my last moments, that the first wife of Napoleon never caused a single tear to flow."

The best service we can render is to live a long and useful life. Who, then, can be sad when the change comes? A pure-souled woman writes about her father, Goff Moore, who recently passed on, laden with the experience of over eighty years, "Yes, I am *glad;* I love him so. Only think of it — eight of father's family over there greeting his arrival."

Catherine H. Fenno, at the ripe age of eighty-six — so writes her son, "A. W. F.," — "a strong-minded woman," was enveloped in a sphere of rest, like that of the Christ, who said, "Father, I have finished the work thou gavest me to do." This is ever the result of a "well spent life ; " and the language is ever like hers : "Let me go home ! "

"In the other life," says Edmund H. Sears, "appears the wonderful paradox that the oldest people are the youngest. To grow in age is to come into everlasting youth. To become old in years is to put on the freshness of perpetual prime. We drop from us the debris of the past ; we breathe the ether of immortality, and our cheeks mantle with eternal bloom."

"You are getting into years." "Yes," replies Gail Hamilton ; "but the years are getting into you ; the ripe, mellow years."

In his rich sermon on "Old Age," Theodore Parker draws this figure, so natural to life : "The stick on his andirons snaps asunder, and falls outward. Two faintly-smoking brands stand there. Grandfather lays them together, and they flame up ; the two smokes are united in one flame. 'Even so let it be in heaven,' says grandfather."

Our American Bryant, now almost the real of the picture he paints, with soul, we trust, white as his snowy locks, is so true to nature : —

"We are not sad to see the gathered grain,
Nor when their mellowed fruits the orchards cast,
Nor when the yellow woods shake down the ripened mast;
We sigh not when the sun, his course fulfilled,
His glowing course, rejoicing earth and sky,

In the soft evening, when the winds are stilled,
  Sinks where his islands of refreshments lie,
And leaves the smile of his departure spread
O'er the warm-colored heaven and ruddy mountain-head.
And I am glad that he survived so long,
  And glad that he has gone to his reward;
Nor can I deem that Nature did him wrong,
  Softly to disengage the vital chord."

Relatively speaking, it is a misfortune to die in childhood or in youth. Children who depart need earth's battles and victories, as the oak the storms, and are unfitted for the lofty uses of ministration until they have served the requisite apprenticeship through secondary mediation, by returning to such homes again, infolded still in the affections of their parents, or such as can nurture them physically, as their chosen matrons do spiritually in the heavenly homes above.

When our beloved have gone, it is a commendable and universal custom to pay respect even to their ashes. But is it worthy of the endearment we feel towards the spirit to have a "funeral parade"? Do you think the risen spirit takes pleasure in seeing show, pomp, and fashion? Is that like heaven, like the ideas of the immortals? The more simple and humble the service, the deeper and sweeter is the spiritual impression. The home, not the church or hall, should be the last place to salute the "clay tenement." Home, where the angel broke the casket and let the prisoner free, is the most appropriate place for the beautiful ceremonies of a funeral. More of soul can be felt there; more of inspiration can come there. That battery for the spirits should not be scattered.

The usual custom, too, of so much staring at the face of the form, sometimes making critical remarks, is reprehensible to a pure, modest taste. Far better would it be for mourners and neighbors and strangers to look beyond that "white veil," to find and see the emancipated spirit.

And shall we put on "mourning," *black* apparel to be in fashion? Is *that* respect for the "gone before?" It is a useless cost and annoyance, especially to the poor. If any outer sign be given, let it be pure white, emblematic of the character we aspire after. A white ribbon, with a sprig of evergreen, would be significant at a funeral; or do as the ancient Greeks, who had, withal, happy views of the "ascended gods," — wear garlands of roses during the days of mourning.

"Kittie" Townsend, a darling little girl in Fond du Lac, Wis., had been instructed by her parents — though she was but six years old — in the beauties of the spiritual gospel, to regard death as beautiful, by which we could the better entertain our angels of the household. Being on a visit in the summer of 1871, to New York State, she there for the first time saw the tenantless form of a sweet child, whose dear mother, a short time before, had passed higher to welcome it to her arms again. It was so beautiful! "Kittie" could not be kept away from it, but from her plays would steal so often alone into that silent room, and hold the child's hand, kiss the pale lips, and then, as if under a seraphic inspiration, talk with the child's spirit about its joy, its flowers up there, its playthings, its pets, its happy mother. Thus the mediumistic Kittie took away all the gloom of death in that bereft home, and brought the angels in, till the place was a "holy of holies."

We love to adorn the dead with the beautiful; it emblemizes to the eye the life beyond. But we err when we try to embalm the "sacred dust," or to lock it up in metallic coffins. Let them be of decayable wood, not black in color, that is gloomy, just like false ideas of death; white is more significant. The sooner the body naturally, not artificially crumbles, the better, to recuperate waste. Let the enriching elements, improved and refined by their former contact with the departed spirit, grow trees and flowers and grasses upon the grave, planted there by some loving hand. Their precious roots will hug that dust so kindly, and our joy will enhance the joy of the recipient plucking the fruit of our fostering, watered by the tears of sympathy. And let us not associate that spot with the dead, but with the living. There is where only the garment was relinquished, when "divine service is over and finished, the chanting hushed, the aisles deserted; and to be contemplated with as little terror and revolting as we gaze at the silent walls of some ruined cathedral."

Victor Hugo, whose soul the immortal poets inspire, paints death in its true light: —

"O, whoever it may be who have seen a beloved being sinking into the tomb, do not think it has left you. The beauty of death is its presence. Inexpressible presence of a soul which smiles upon our tearful eyes. The being that we mourn has disappeared, but has not departed. We no longer see its gentle face, but we feel that wave beneath its wings. The dead are invisible, but they are not absent. Let us be just to death. Let us not be ungrateful to death. It is not, as has been said, a ruin and a snare. It is an error to think that here in the darkness of the open grave all is lost to us. There everything is found again. The grave is a place of restitution; there the soul resumes the infinite, there it recovers its plenitude. There it re-enters on the possession of all its mysterious nature; it is set free from the body, from want, from its burden, from fatality. Death is the greatest of liberties; it is also the furthest progress. Death is a higher step for all who have lived upon its height. Dazzling and holy every one receives his increase, everything is transfigured in the light and by the light. He who has been no more than virtuous on earth becomes beauteous; he who has only been beauteous becomes sublime; and he who has only been sublime becomes good."

Better is it to celebrate one's departure than physical birth. This was a memorable custom with the early spiritual Christians and classic Greeks and Romans. It should be renewed each year, as a "spiritual anniversary," to keep fresh in remembrance the virtues and beatitudes of our dear departed. "Not by lamentations and mournful chants," says Plutarch, "ought we to celebrate the funerals of the good, but by hymns; for in ceasing to be numbered with mortals, they enter upon the heritage of a diviner life."

We should avoid probing yet deeper the sensitive weepers. Ours should be the work of *healing*, not of wounding. The hollow sound of dirt *shovelled* upon the coffin, when lowered into its narrow house, grates upon the ear. It would seem as if our customs were instituted by those who delight in torture. Let the sounds then be words of cheer, sweet words of sympathy, and enlivening, inspiring songs. Throwing sprigs of evergreen and flowers upon those "sacred ashes" is more in keeping with the soul's sense of propriety and respect.

The custom once was, in the days of ignorance, for the minister to harrow up the feelings of the mourners as much as possible, by gloomy pictures of death, as an incentive to repentance. Such groaning even the beasts are not guilty of. Whilst there is pensive feeling, let it be the aim of the minister or speaker to render the services short, beautiful, and inspiring. Only those who have tasted of the "heavenly manna" mediumistically, who *know* something by experience of the world to come, are qualified to instruct and console the bereft and sorrowing. The person best qualified to speak a few words of comfort to the bereft is some dear friend or relative who is intimately acquainted with the "gone before." Then it is a home feeling. Open then the windows at the dome of the soul; let the light enter; look over and up into the great splendor of the immortal world, and tears will glisten with hope, and within the affections will rest the dove of the spirit.

From the portals, which our beloved passed, unharmed by the damp and decay that again feed the living; from the lovely home altars rusted with our tears, from the sad yet beautiful scenes of parting, let us turn to the new drama of existence, ourselves actors too, to reveal the *good* and *holy*, hidden beyond this attenuating veil. Patience, tired pilgrims! Light from heaven is calm. As the beautiful of nature in flower and tree, lake and hill, refines the mind and thence its body, so association with angels moulds us in their fair likenesses. Wherever they glide is left a trail of heavenly light. "How beautiful upon the mountains are the feet of him that bringeth good tidings of good, that publisheth peace!"

Every moment we are physically wasting or dying, yet living on the same identities. We recognize each other by soul emotions. Even if friends have lived apart for years — if death divide them — by touch of spheres we are recognized. Identity is a law of spiritual species; and how delicate is its action! The soul applies its measure; and if love comes with the step, or voice, or look, it is "meeting in heaven." Play upon a piano near a well-toned guitar, and the one responds to the other. It is piano music, but a guitar voice. The two instruments blend their melodies. When we are good enough, and calm as a cloudless night of stars, we can go up into an orchestra of souls, and, as angels from earth and spirit lands greet each other again by familiar emotions, stirred by the rushing lights of minds that are kindred with our own; and O, the music of that oratorio! the deep harmony of that recognition! By this inward touch of soul with soul, we "know each other there" as here, when in a moment all the reminiscences of the past spring into conscious being, embossed in the resplendent glory of immortality, till even earth's mistakes now righted are mere beautiful colorings in our robes of character.

Clear truth is set in the laws of life's philosophy. The scientists of the ages have revealed it. Our Tyndalls and Lockyers, by a delicate adjustment of machinery to "catch a sunbeam," have analyzed its elemental ingredients. If a ray casts the same shadowy circle as hydrogen when burned, that ray is hydrogenic. A closer analysis will reveal all the solar constituents; and thence their native soils, waters, and atmospheres, and the inhabitants peopling that strange orb with its grades of civilization. Does not the least particle represent the nature of the whole? An Agassiz will construct an artificial skeleton of an extinct animal from a single bone, exactly as the creature was. A skilful physiognomist, from the sight of a hand only, will analyze the make-up of its owner. A psychometrist, from a lock of hair, or a letter, will trace the character and life history of its possessor. Our media, more scientific than they seem, living closer to the realm of causation, indicate in their powers of mind the influence of an unseen world upon them. As Professor Winchell, of the University of Michigan, says,—

"The unseen world is destined to become like a newly discovered continent. We shall visit it; we shall hold communion with it; we shall wonder how so many thousand years could have passed without our being introduced to it. We shall learn of other modes of existence, — intermediate, perhaps, between body and spirit — having the forms and limitations in space peculiar to matter, with the penetrability and invisibility of spirit. And who can say that we may not yet obtain such knowledge of the modes of existence of other bodies as to discover the means of rendering them visible to our bodily eyes, as we now hold conversation with a friend upon the shores of the Pacific, or in the heart of Europe, or fly with the superhuman velocity of the wind from the Atlantic to the Mississippi valley? Then may we not at last gaze upon the spiritual bodies in which our departed friends reside, and discover the means of listening to their spirit voices, and join hands consciously with the heavenly host?"

Those voices *we* hear, those faces we see, those hands we touch. Divine *reality! Golden* is the soul-breathed thought that inspired the mind of the ascended Mrs. Booth, published in Theodore Tilton's Golden Age: —

"I feel a soft hand on my head,
A hand whose touch seems overspread
With balm like that the lilies shed
O'er the white bosoms of the dead,
And I am chill while memories fall
Like odors o'er me — that is all.

"I feel the rhythm and the rhyme
Of thy dear life keep sweetest time
With God's sweet sounds, and overclimb
All sounds with which they interchime.
I see thee — hear thee — feel thy breath,
In the still air which answereth
With lightest kiss whene'er I call,
'Mid tears for thee — and this is all."

"It doth not yet appear what we shall be," said the beloved disciple. Truly so; we know not the extent of our work or influence. We *now* may have an unbalanced organism, which compels us to battle with self and the world; and the superficial multitude may classify us as "sinful," when in fact the soul *may* be struggling for supremacy. The *purpose* to overcome, though we may not to-day reach the goal, will, if repeated again and again, constitute a confirmed act of virtue in the "inner life." The skill we show in our works cannot be the full measure of our genius. How few can express in song or word what they feel! We are all conscious of an "imprisoned fulness." What if our productions are defective and rejected in earth's markets; the will to do and the deed accomplished are wares that sell well in the markets of the "City of God." The angels appreciate a finish, and cease not their discipline over us until the external is the fac-simile of the internal; but soul is their pupil; and when this is active for good and purity, there is joy in heaven, though weeping on earth over failures. The eternal angel within is fashioned by ways not known, but rather discarded in our philosophies of etiquette. Courage! poor woman, bowed with care, sorrowing over the departure of all thy loved ones for the other home, leaving thee a riven monument of thy former grace and beauty; that look upward, that tear from a pure crystal fount, that voice of tenderness, that ear of pity, that defence of the wronged, are golden steps higher.

O, orphan child! so homeless, so forlorn, so unreprieved; the little child-angels have *not* forsaken thee, nor has thy mother, early gone, — she is drawing thee fast to her arms of love again, for "it doth not yet appear what we shall be." O, weary mortals, blasted in expectations, grieved over buried hopes, wrecked in the adventure for gain, — look up! There *is* a beacon star shining through all this darkness — there is a light beyond — there is a voice shouting in this dread silence — there is a hand to lead you safe over the billow, the moment a prayer of feeling, uttered or unuttered, trembles forth, reporting to the watch-angels the need of help.

Yes, the dear one returns, and unlocks the treasury of memory. The cradle, the lullaby song, the garden, the brook, the maple tree, the birds that sang in it, the old armed-chair, the mother's anxious prayer, the father's pride, the school-house and church, the play-times with the boys and girls long ago, the sorrows and joys, the mistakes and victories, the sicknesses and bereavements, the "good by" and the "greeting," all are remembered then — all seem then as life-chords to the soul, pulsing up to us the loves of other days, and leading us forward into new experiences, intertwining and blending in sweet accord — the past lived again, this time regenerated — the future but the light of which earth is the shadow cast into the focus of the living present; and we hear and we *see*, not by *faith* alone, but by *knowledge* of continuous and ever-blessed association with God's great angels; and O, the heights and depths of the glory all around, of the glory all along the pilgrim-way!

If the price of this joy is the price of self-denial, of earth-partings amid tearful baptisms, that "purify the heart and overcome the world," how gladly should we pay it! If such a price add also to the joy of our beloved, what should hinder us from securing "the prize of this high calling"?

www.ingramcontent.com/pod-product-compliance
Lightning Source LLC
LaVergne TN
LVHW021430110826
845150LV00007B/2175

* 9 7 8 1 4 2 5 5 0 6 6 9 8 *